CAMBRIDGE LIBRARY COLLECTION

Books of enduring scholarly value

British and Irish History, Seventeenth and Eighteenth Centuries

The books in this series focus on the British Isles in the early modern period, as interpreted by eighteenth- and nineteenth-century historians, and show the shift to 'scientific' historiography. Several of them are devoted exclusively to the history of Ireland, while others cover topics including economic history, foreign and colonial policy, agriculture and the industrial revolution. There are also works in political thought and social theory, which address subjects such as human rights, the role of women, and criminal justice.

The Rural Economy of the West of England

Between 1787 and 1798, the agricultural writer and land agent William Marshall (1745–1818) published a number of works on the rural economies of England, covering Norfolk, his native Yorkshire, Gloucestershire, the Midlands and the South. This two-volume study appeared in 1796 and investigated the farming, geography, public works and produce of districts in Devon, Somerset, Dorset and Cornwall. Volume 1 looks in detail at West Devon, the eastern parts of Cornwall, and the South Hams. The coverage includes aspects of the laws surrounding land ownership, farming implements peculiar to the areas, woodland management, orchards and the production of fruit-based liquors. The result is a richly detailed survey of the area in the Georgian period and an important record of rural and agricultural life, so often overlooked by other contemporary chroniclers.

Cambridge University Press has long been a pioneer in the reissuing of out-of-print titles from its own backlist, producing digital reprints of books that are still sought after by scholars and students but could not be reprinted economically using traditional technology. The Cambridge Library Collection extends this activity to a wider range of books which are still of importance to researchers and professionals, either for the source material they contain, or as landmarks in the history of their academic discipline.

Drawing from the world-renowned collections in the Cambridge University Library and other partner libraries, and guided by the advice of experts in each subject area, Cambridge University Press is using state-of-the-art scanning machines in its own Printing House to capture the content of each book selected for inclusion. The files are processed to give a consistently clear, crisp image, and the books finished to the high quality standard for which the Press is recognised around the world. The latest print-on-demand technology ensures that the books will remain available indefinitely, and that orders for single or multiple copies can quickly be supplied.

The Cambridge Library Collection brings back to life books of enduring scholarly value (including out-of-copyright works originally issued by other publishers) across a wide range of disciplines in the humanities and social sciences and in science and technology.

The Rural Economy of the West of England

Including Devonshire, and Parts of Somersetshire, Dorsetshire, and Cornwall

VOLUME 1

WILLIAM MARSHALL

CAMBRIDGE
UNIVERSITY PRESS

University Printing House, Cambridge, CB2 8BS, United Kingdom

Published in the United States of America by Cambridge University Press, New York

Cambridge University Press is part of the University of Cambridge.
It furthers the University's mission by disseminating knowledge in the pursuit of education, learning and research at the highest international levels of excellence.

www.cambridge.org
Information on this title: www.cambridge.org/9781108067539

This edition first published 1796
This digitally printed version 2014

ISBN 978-1-108-06753-9 Paperback

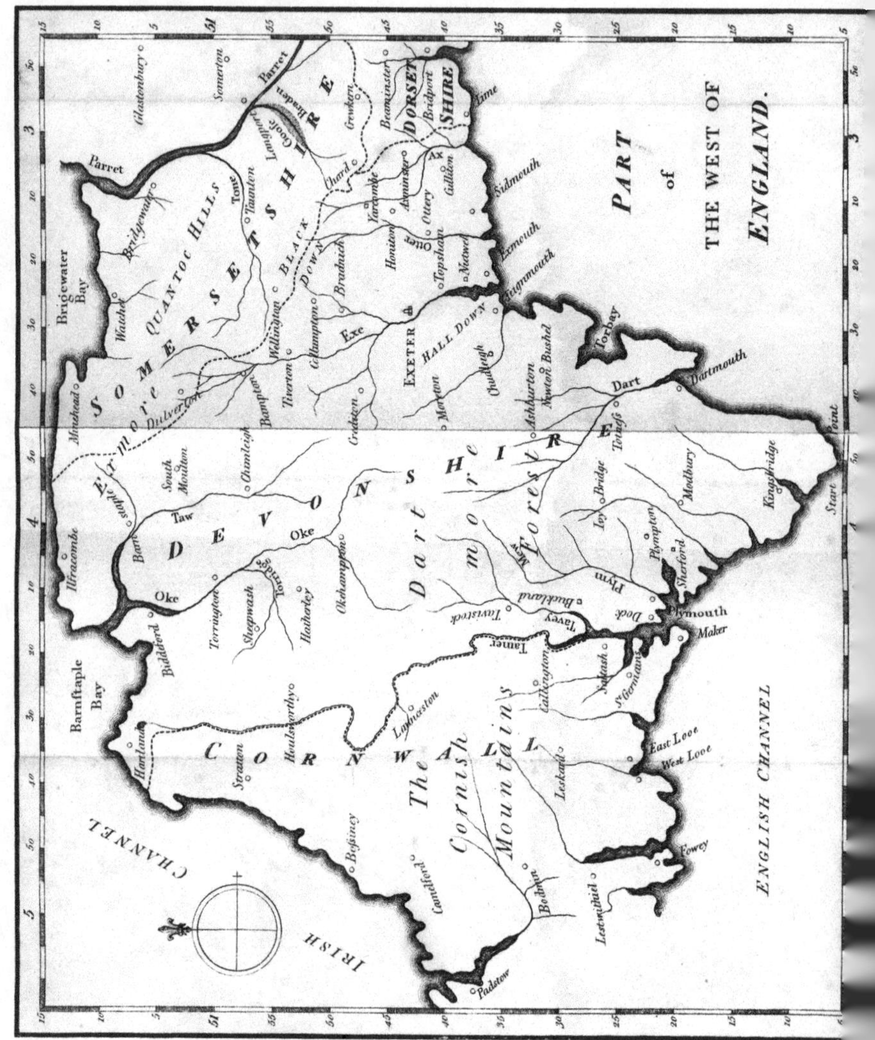

The material originally positioned here is too large for reproduction in this reissue. A PDF can be downloaded from the web address given on page iv of this book, by clicking on 'Resources Available'.

THE
RURAL ECONOMY
OF THE
WEST OF ENGLAND:

INCLUDING

DEVONSHIRE;

AND PARTS OF

SOMERSETSHIRE,
DORSETSHIRE,

AND

CORNWALL.

TOGETHER WITH

MINUTES IN PRACTICE.

By Mr. MARSHALL.

IN TWO VOLUMES.

VOL. I.

LONDON:
Printed for G. NICOL, Bookseller to His Majesty, Pall Mall;
G. G. and J. ROBINSON, Paternoster Row;
and J. DEBRETT, Piccadilly.

M,DCC,XCVI.

CONTENTS

OF THE

FIRST VOLUME.

THE

WEST OF ENGLAND.

DISTRICT THE FIRST.

WEST DEVONSHIRE, &c.

Hun-

THE

THE RURAL ECONOMY OF *THIS DISTRICT*.

DIVISION THE FIRST.

LANDED ESTATES, AND THEIR MANAGEMENT.

DIVISION

DIVISION THE SECOND.

WOODLANDS,

THEIR

PROPAGATION AND MANAGEMENT.

DIVISION THE THIRD.

AGRICULTURE.

SECT.

4. Pressing,

South

DISTRICT THE SECOND.

THE SOUTH HAMS OF DEVONSHIRE.

The AGRICULTURE of this Diſtrict.

RETROSPECTIVE

RETROSPECTIVE VIEW

OF

SOUTH DEVONSHIRE.

ADVER-

ADVERTISEMENT.

A PERIOD of almoſt ſix years has elapſed, ſince the publication of the Rural Practice of the MIDLAND COUNTIES. The proſecution of the General Work, of which that publication makes a part, has not, however, been neglected, during this lapſe of time. The Practices of the MORE WESTERN COUNTIES have been regiſtered, and are here offered to the Public. And thoſe of the SOUTHERN COUNTIES have been examined and collected *.

I HAVE,

* And will be digeſted, and publiſhed, with ſuitable diſpatch.

I HAVE, therefore, at length obtained a GENERAL VIEW of the ESTABLISHED PRACTICES of ENGLAND. And, altho' I have had a partial View of those of SCOTLAND, it is not my intention to extend my Remarks to that part of the Island, or to WALES, until I have, in some measure, *rounded my plan*, with respect to ENGLAND.

SINCE the Publication of the RURAL ECONOMY of the MIDLAND COUNTIES, a BOARD OF AGRICULTURE has been appointed, and a Plan of Survey, similar to my own, has been adopted circumstances which caused some apprehension, in my friends, and a degree of alarm, in my Booksellers, lest the REPORTS of the Board should supersede the use of the REGISTERS I had published, and should render abortive an undertaking, on which I had expended the most valuable part of life.

I CONFESS,

I CONFESS, that when I ventured to recommend to public attention, the Eſtabliſhment of a Board of Agriculture *, it did

* In the following paſſage, publiſhed (in 1790) in the RURAL ECONOMY of the MIDLAND COUNTIES, i. 222.

" I have already ſaid, in the courſe of this work, that it " is not my intention to obtrude my ſentiments, un- " ſeemingly, on NATIONAL CONCERNS; but poſſeſſed " of the maſs of information, which, in the nature of my " purſuit, I muſt neceſſarily have accumulated,—no man, " *perhaps*, having had a ſimilar opportunity,—I think it a " duty I owe to ſociety, and an inſeparable part of my " preſent undertaking, to regiſter ſuch ideas, whether " political or profeſſional, as reſult, aptly and fairly, out " of the ſubject before me: and, in this place, I think it " right to intimate the probable advantage which might " ariſe from a BOARD OF AGRICULTURE;—or, more " generally, of RURAL AFFAIRS; to take cognizance, " not of the ſtate and promotion of AGRICULTURE, " merely; but alſo of the CULTIVATION OF WASTES and " the PROPAGATION OF TIMBER: baſes on which, not " Commerce only, but the political exiſtence of the Nation " is founded. And when may this Country expect a " more favorable opportunity, than the preſent, of laying " a broad and firm baſis of its future proſperity?"

Here, I find my pen forcibly arreſted, and bent from the public ſervice, towards my own gratification. And it may be pardonable in a man, who has labored long and hard in the ſervice of the Public, and this, too, with but few

did not occur to me, that ſuch an inſtitution would, in any way, interfere with my own undertaking,---and much leſs, that it would become a valuable ſource of information, moſt happily calculated to promote it.

BUT finding the meaſure of provincial ſurveys adopted, and ſeeing the public benefit it was capable of producing, I was among the firſt to comply with the requeſt of my honorable Friend, the PRESIDENT OF THE BOARD, --- whoſe public ſpirit entitles him to every attention, --- and to furniſh

few gratifications, except what have occaſionally riſen from his own reflections, to indulge himſelf, for once, in ſuffering his reflections to force their way into public notice—and to ſuggeſt—that had the GENERAL BILL OF INCLOSURE, which he earneſtly recommended, in 1788 (ſee the RURAL ECONOMY of YORKSHIRE, VOL. I. Page 101.), been preſently paſſed into a law, and had a BOARD of AGRICULTURE been inſtituted, in 1790, and DULY ENCOURAGED, it is more than probable, that the diſtreſſing ſcarcity, which this Country experienced, in the ſummer of 1795, would not now have lain a reproach, on the POLITICAL ECONOMY of the Iſland.

furnish my quota of information; by presenting to the Board a REPORT of the CENTRAL HIGHLANDS of Scotland;--- where I was resident, at the time of its establishment: and this I did, under the natural impression, that I was, in effect, working in my own field, and with fellow laborers, who were jointly employed, in collecting facts, that could not fail of proving useful, to the GENERAL WORK, which has ever been the EVENTUAL OBJECT of my Undertaking *.

IT did not, however, strike me, at that time, as it has done since, that the Board's Reports may be rendered more immediately serviceable to my Work, in assisting to fill up the vacant interstices of my Registers; and thereby to make them more worthy, than otherwise they would have been, of the

* See the prefatory ADVERTISEMENT to the RURAL ECONOMY of NORFOLK, for the outlines of this Undertaking.

the title I wish them collectively to deserve; — namely, AN AUTHENTIC REGISTER OF THE RURAL ECONOMY OF ENGLAND, AT THE CLOSE OF THE EIGHTEENTH CENTURY.

To my valuable and lamented friend, the late SIR FRANCIS DRAKE, whose virtues were best known to those who were best acquainted with his private character, I am chiefly indebted for the opportunity of forming the Register, which is now under publication.

IN the Summer of 1791, I made my first journey into the WEST of DEVONSHIRE, to examine into the state of his Rural concerns, in that part of the County; and, in the Autumn of the same year, returned,

turned, to endeavour to retrieve them from the disgraceful state, in which I had found them. In the succeeding Autumn, I made a third journey, to the same quarter; and, in the Summer of 1794, I went over the whole of the DRAKE ESTATE, lying in different parts of Devonshire.

IT will perhaps be said, that the VALLEY OF THE TAMER, is too confined, and is of too little importance as a District, to be suitable for a PRINCIPAL STATION. Indeed, it is more than probable, that had I *chosen* my station, it would not have been that which circumstances assigned me.

BUT (thanks to the Disposer of Circumstances),—now, when I am acquainted with the several Districts of this Department of the Island, I am convinced, that there is no other situation, which could have been

been made equally favorable to my views, as that in which I was placed—*as it were* providentially. There is no other individual station, in which I could have commanded, so well, the two Counties of DEVON and CORNWALL, and, at the same time, the fertile District of the SOUTH HAMS,—"the Garden of Devonshire,"—of which distinguished District the Valley of the Tamer forms, in reality, a part.

BESIDE, in the Valley of the Tamer, and on the magnificent Farm on which I resided,—the very first in the Country,—I possessed the most favorable opportunity, that either circumstances or choice had to give, of studying the DANMONIAN PRACTICE, in all its branches, and in its almost pristine purity *.

A FEW

* DANMONIAN,—an epithet derived from DANMONIA, the antient name of part, or the whole, of this Western Peninsula of Britain.

A FEW particulars of modern practice, that have been recently introduced into this part of the Island, especially into the South Hams, have not deranged the LONG-ESTABLISHED SYSTEM OF DANMONIAN HUSBANDRY; which is still firmly rooted, in the several Districts of this Department; and remains as distinguishable from the ordinary management of the body of the Island, as if the Peninsula, they form, had been recently attached to it.

MOREOVER, it will appear, in the following pages, that, although the Danmonian practice has many defects, it has likewise its excellencies, by which the British Husbandman may greatly profit; and very many peculiarities, by which the mind of an attentive reader will be enlarged, and its prejudices be relaxed. I there-

I therefore consider it as one of the most fortunate circumstances, that have attended the execution of my undertaking, that I was led to the pure fountain of this distinguished practice.

LONDON, May, 1796.

THE

WEST OF ENGLAND.

INTRODUCTORY REMARKS.

THIS popular appellation is usually given to the four most Western Counties; namely, CORNWALL, DEVONSHIRE, SOMERSETSHIRE, and DORSETSHIRE.

But, in examining a Country, like England, with a view to the existing state of its AGRICULTURE, and the other branches of its RURAL ECONOMY, the arbitrary lines of Counties are to be wholly disregarded. For if any plan was observed in determining the outlines of Provinces, in this Island, it certainly had no reference or alliance whatever to Agriculture; unless it were to divide, between opposing claimants, the natural Diſtricts, which require to be ſtudied ſeparately, and entire. *Natural*, not *fortuitous* lines, are requiſite to be traced; *Agricultural*, not *political* diſtinctions, are to be regarded.

A NATURAL DISTRICT is marked by a uniformity or ſimilarity of SOIL and SURFACE; whether, by ſuch uniformity, a marſh, a vale, an extent of upland, a range of chalky heights, or a ſtretch of barren mountains, be produced. And an AGRICULTURAL DISTRICT is diſcriminated by a uniformity or ſimilarity of PRACTICE; whether it be characteriſed by grazing, ſheep farming, arable management, or mixed cultivation; or by the production of ſome particular article, as dairy produce, fruit liquor, &c. &c.

Now, it is evident, that the boundary lines of Counties pay no regard to theſe circumſtances. On the contrary, we frequently find the moſt entire Diſtricts, with reſpect to Nature and Agriculture, ſevered by political lines of demarcation. The Midland Diſtricts, for inſtance, a whole with reſpect to ſoil, ſurface, and eſta-

eſtabliſhed practice, is reduced to mere fragments, by the outlines of the four Counties of Leiceſter, Warwick, Stafford, and Derby *. Again, The Fruit Liquor Diſtrict of the Wye and Severn includes parts of the Counties of Hereford, Glouceſter, and Worceſter †; and the Dairy Diſtrict of North Wiltſhire receives portions of the Counties of Glouceſter and Berkſhire within its limits, and extends its practice to the Eaſtern margin of Somerſetſhire ‡.

Hence, it may be truly ſaid, to proſecute an Agricultural Survey, by Counties, is to ſet at naught the diſtinctions of Nature, which it is the intention of the Surveyor to examine and deſcribe; and to ſeparate into parts the diſtinguiſhed practices, which it is his buſineſs to regiſter entire.

SUCH a mode of procedure is not only an impropriety in theory, but in practice. It deſtroys that SIMPLICITY of EXECUTION and PERSPICUITY OF ARRANGEMENT,

* See RUR. ECON. of the MIDLAND COUNTIES.

† See GLO. ECON.

‡ See as above.

MENT, which alone can render an extensive undertaking pleasurable to him who prosecutes it, and profitable to the Public.

Another practical objection, which lies against surveying by Counties, beside the repetitions or references it requires, is the UNNECESSARY LABOR it incurs, and the SUPERFLUOUS VOLUMES it necessarily gives rise to. For it is not the practice of every township or farm, which *can* be registered, nor that of every hundred or county, which *requires* it.

It is the SUPERIOR PRACTICES of DISTINGUISHED NATURAL DISTRICTS, in different and DISTANT PARTS OF THE ISLAND (thus separating its more DISTINCT PRACTICES), and these only, that are necessary to be fixed; AS A FIRM BASIS, ON WHICH TO RAISE FUTURE IMPROVEMENTS, AND STILL MORE ENLIGHTENED PRACTICES. The intermediate lands either partake of the management of these distinguished Districts, or are subjected to methods that are less eligible; and are therefore not requisite to be registered.

The

The DISTRICTS of the WEST OF ENGLAND, which require to be deſcribed or noticed in this regiſter are,

Firſt, WEST DEVONSHIRE, or THE VALLEY OF THE TAMER: including the Weſtern Margin of Devonſhire, and the Eaſtern parts of Cornwall.

Second, The SOUTH HAMS. A contiguous Diſtrict, which forms the Southern point of Devonſhire.

Third, The MOUNTAINS of Cornwall and Devonſhire.

Fourth, The Diſtrict of NORTH DEVONSHIRE.

Fifth, THE VALE OF EXETER.

Sixth, The DAIRY DISTRICT, which includes parts of Eaſt Devonſhire and Weſt Dorſetſhire;—and,

Seventh, The VALE OF TAUNTON, in Somerſetſhire.

DISTRICT THE FIRST.

WEST DEVONSHIRE;

INCLUDING

THE EASTERN PARTS

OF

CORNWALL.

INTRODUCTORY VIEW OF THIS DISTRICT.

BEFORE we enter into a detail of the ſeveral branches of the RURAL ECONOMY of the Diſtrict of Weſt Devonſhire, &c. it will be requiſite to take a comprehenſive view of the DISTRICT itſelf; and to endeavour to mark its diſtinguiſhing characters.

FIRST, As a production of Nature.

SECONDLY, As part of the domain of the realm.

THIRDLY, As the property of individuals.

SECTION THE FIRST.

NATURAL CHARACTERISTICS OF WEST DEVONSHIRE, &c.

IN taking a cursory view of the NATURAL HISTORY of this District, I shall attend to such particulars, only, as have an immediate connection with RURAL ECONOMICS; conformably with the plan which I have hitherto found it requisite to pursue. These particulars are,

I. Its situation in the Island.

II. Its extent.

III. Its elevation with respect to the sea.

IV. The conformation of its surface.

V. Its climature as it affects Agriculture.

VI. The waters which occupy its surface.

VII. Its prevailing ſoils.

VIII. The ſubſoils moſt prevalent.

IX. The uſeful foſſils found in its ſubſtrata.

X. The minerals it contains.

I. The SITUATION of this Diſtrict is within the South-weſtern limb of the Iſland, which ſeparates the two ſeas—the Iriſh and the Engliſh Channels.

Its NATURAL BOUNDARIES are Dartmore, an extenſive and elevated tract of mountains, on the Eaſt; Hingſtone, and other mountains of Cornwall, on the Weſt; with Plymouth Sound, and the eſtuaries branching out of it, on the South. The Northern boundary is leſs evident. Brent Tor and the heaths around it may be ſaid to ſeparate this Diſtrict from NORTH DEVONSHIRE.

II. The EXTENT of this ſecluded tract of country is not inconſiderable: It is about twenty miles from North to South, and about ten miles from Eaſt to Weſt.

Weſt. But within theſe limits ſome barren lands are included.

III. Its ELEVATION above the ſea is leſs than the eye may eſtimate. The tide flows to its center. The vallies of courſe lie low; but the hills riſe abruptly; and much of the cultivated lands may be deemed *hill*; all of them *upland*. No part of the Diſtrict can be ſtrictly called vale; nor is there any extent of flat meadows, or marſh lands, within it; though, here and there, a narrow bottom or "coombe" is obſervable: theſe meadowy ſlips, probably, having been formed by the waters which now ſkirt them.

IV. The SURFACE is various in the extreme: not only from the number, narrowneſs, and depth of the larger vallies, whoſe ſides generally riſe ſteeply from the banks of the ſtreams that divide them; but from the hills, or wider ſpaces between thoſe vallies, being rent and broken, in the manner peculiar to the South-weſtern extremity of the Iſland: a ſtyle of ſurface which takes place at the Weſtern termination

nation of the chalk hills of Dorſetſhire, and continues to the Landsend.

V. The CLIMATURE of Weſt Devonſhire is particularly marked. The ſituation of the Diſtrict between two ſeas; its immediate expoſure to the main ocean, in the direct paſſage of the South-weſt winds, and the elevated ſummits of the mountains, which ſurround it, arreſting the fleets of vapours as they arrive heavy laden from the Atlantic, unite in rendering this portion of the Iſland liable to an exceſs of rain; this, to a coolneſs of climature, and a lateneſs of ſeaſon. Though ſituated in the moſt Southern *climate* of the Iſland, its harveſts are comparatively late; but vary in a ſingular manner with the ſeaſon.

In 1791, wheat crops in general were green, the firſt of *Auguſt*, and hay harveſt was, then, barely at its height. The twenty-fifth of Auguſt, corn harveſt was in forwardneſs, the weather having recently been dry and hot. Nevertheleſs, at that time, much corn ſtill remained green; eſpecially on on the ſkirts of the Corniſh mountains, where wheat is not unfrequently harveſted after Michaelmas. In 1792, barley harveſt did not cloſe, even on the comparatively forward lands of Buckland Place, until the beginning of October: the ſeaſon wet. On the contrary, in 1794, a very dry ſeaſon, wheat harveſt commenced the laſt week in July.

Taking the par of years, we may fairly place Weſt Devonſhire ten days or a fortnight behind the Midland Diſtrict, which lies more than two degrees of *latitude*—namely, about one hundred and fifty ſtatute miles—farther North. A proof that *climate* and *climature* have not an immediate connection.

VI. WATERS. This Diſtrict, notwithſtanding the ſteepneſs and elevation of its ſurface, is ſingularly well watered. Every deſcription of water may be ſaid to belong to it, except the lake.

The SEA and its ESTUARIES ſever it to its center. Its RIVERS are the *Tamer*, the *Tavey*, and the *Plym*; whoſe various brooks,

brooks, rivulets, and rills, furrow the ſides of almoſt every ſlope; frequently iſſuing from near the ſummits of the hills.

But I have met with no inſtance of collected waters, among the Weſtern mountains; ſuch as frequently occur in the Northern parts of the Iſland. Doſmary Pool, a ſmall lakelet, which lies among the mountains, between Bodmin and Launceſton, is the only one I have ſeen.

It is among complex ranges of mountains that lakes are generally found. Thoſe of Cornwall and Devonſhire form only one chain, except in the part where this pool occurs.

VII. SOILS. The SPECIES of ſurface ſoil is remarkably uniform, and ſingular in its component parts. It does not claſs properly with any of the ordinary deſcriptions of ſoils, namely, clay, loam, ſand, or gravel; but is rather of a ſilty nature. Perhaps the principal part of the ordinary ſoil of the Diſtrict is periſhed ſlate-ſtone rubble; or ſlate ſtone itſelf, reduced by the action of the atmoſphere to its original ſilt or mud: among which, however, a

portion

portion of loamy mold is mixed, in various degrees of quantity.

Hence, though the ſpecies of ſoil may be ſaid to be the ſame, the QUALITY varies, and in ſome inſtances, very greatly. There are ſmall plots of land, upon the upper branches of the Tavey, equal in quality with the beſt-ſoiled Diſtricts of the Iſland; deep rich land; grazing ground of the firſt quality.

The prevailing DEPTHS of the ſoils of the ordinary cultivated lands of the Diſtrict are, from five to ten inches. But they are ſeldom free from rocks or large ſtones to theſe depths: and they are generally mixed plentifully with looſe fragments of ſimilar rocks and ſtones: of which, under the next head.

Other obſervable circumſtances of the ſoils of Weſt Devonſhire reſpect their ABSORBENCY, and their being in a manner free from TENACITY. For, notwithſtanding their ſmoothneſs, and apparent unctuouſneſs while wet, they preſently become dry and clean, after the heavieſt rain: excepting after a long continuance of of winter rains, when, the ſubſoil being ſurcharged, the ſoil, eſpecially in particular plots, remains perhaps, for ſome length of time, in a ſtate of mud; yielding to the foot in walking over it; a mere quagmire; horſes and cattle reaching the rocky ſubſtratum every ſtep. This evil quality, however, is narrowly limited, both in reſpect to extent and continuance; and might be removed, by draining.

Upon the whole, the natural properties of this ſingular ſpecies of ſoil is ſuch, as to render it highly favorable to the purpoſes of Huſbandry; as being, under proper treatment, productive either of corn or graſs.

VIII. SUBSOIL. This is univerſally of a ſtony nature. I met with no beds of clay, loam, ſand, or gravel; ſuch as we find in other Diſtricts. The prevailing ſubſtratum is a ſoft SLATEY ROCK; which, in ſome places, riſes to the ſoil; in others intervenes a ſtratum of rubble, or unhardened ſlate; which, in quality, partakes of the firmer and purer rock; the relation of the two being analogous with that which ſub-

ſubſiſts between limeſtone and the rubble, with which it is frequently covered *.

Intermixed with the ſoil, and often united with fragments of ſlate rock, is found, in blocks and fragments of various ſizes, a ſpecies of cryſtal, or quartz—provincially "WHITTAKER;" which, in colour, is moſtly white, ſometimes tinged with red, or ruſt colour.

Obſerving, in ſeveral ſpecimens of this foſſil, ſome reſemblance of gypſum; and alſo remarking the fertilizing quality of the waters which filter through theſe ſlatey rocks: and moreover finding them inſenſible to the marine acid, uſed as a teſt; I was led to the idea, that they were of a gypſeous nature.

To endeavour to aſcertain the component parts of the SLATE ROCK, of which the hills of the cultivated parts of the Diſtrict may be ſaid to be formed, I ſubjected different ſpecimens† of it to an extended courſe of

* See YORK ECON. Vol. I. page 336.

† Theſe ſpecimens were the ordinary BUILDING STONE of Buckland Place, and the COVERING SLATE of a quarry

of experiments; which I proſecuted with greater ſolicitude, as I had been informed, by an authority which I conceived to admit not of doubt, that the Weſtmorland ſlate contains a conſiderable proportion of calcareous earth in its compoſition, and I was deſirous to aſcertain whether the ſlate of Devonſhire, whoſe appearances are ſimilar, were not likewiſe ſimilar in component parts.

All that requires to be ſaid, in this place, reſpecting theſe experiments, is, that the ſlate rock of Weſt Devonſhire appears, from their ſeveral reſults, to be void of calcareous earth, in a ſtate of gypſum, and that the proportion it contains of this earth, in a ſtate of chalk, is very ſmall.

It may, however, be right to add here, that, on extending the experiments to the RUBBLE, and the CHRYSTAL, abovementioned, they appear to have been formed from the ſame materials with the rock itſelf.

a quarry in its neighbourhood. They appear to be only varieties of the ſame ſpecies of foſſil; and might, no doubt, be traced, by connected gradations, into each other.

itſelf. The former contains the ingredients of ſlate, in a looſe impure form: and the latter, part of the ſame ingredients, in a purer ſtate.

IX. FOSSILS. BLUE SLATES of the firſt quality, for covering houſes, are raiſed in different parts of the Diſtrict. SLATE STONES, for walling, are formed in moſt parts of it.

A ſingular ſpecies of FREESTONE is found near the center of this Diſtrict. It has formerly been diſtributed over the Weſt of Devonſhire, and a great part of Cornwall; having been uſed moſt eſpecially for ſculptural purpoſes, in the Gothic ornaments of churches and other buildings. It appears to have received its immediate formation from fire; though evidently not the production of a volcano, in the ſituation in which it is now found; being ſcattered, at preſent, in detached rocks. It is called "Rooborough ſtone," from the name of the common paſture on which it is more particularly or principally found *. MOOR-STONE

* It is inſenſible to the marine acid.

STONE or QUARTZOSE GRANITE is plentifully found, on either ſide of the Diſtrict.

X. MINERALS. Mines of TIN, COPPER, and LEAD (containing a portion of SILVER) are ſtill worked in the Diſtrict; whoſe ſurface is defaced, and for ever rendered unprofitable, for the purpoſes of agriculture and cultivation, by theſe intolerable peſts. The ſtannary laws, if any ſuch laws can really be ſaid to exiſt, ought to be forthwith abrogated, and ſome rational regulations be ſtruck out;—ſuch as men of common ſenſe may underſtand, and under which induſtry may be protected, from the rapine of adventurers; who, not unfrequently, do irreparable injury, without obtaining any counter advantage to themſelves or the community: throwing away that attention and labor, which, if beſtowed on the ſoil, might remain an everlaſting benefit.

SECTION THE SECOND.

THE PRESENT STATE OF THE DISTRICT AS A PART OF THE NATIONAL DOMAIN.

IN viewing what may be termed the POLITICAL ECONOMY of this Diſtrict, it may be proper to confine ourſelves to the following branches of that ſubject.

I. The political Diviſions of the Diſtrict.

II. The preſent ſtate of Society within it.

III. The public works it poſſeſſes.

IV. Its preſent productions, as they may be viewed in a political light.

V. The characteriſtic features, or the preſent appearance of the face of the country, viewed as a paſſage or part of the demeſne lands of the Empire.

I. POLI-

I. POLITICAL DIVISIONS. The COUNTY of Devon ranks among the largeſt of the Engliſh Counties.

In regulating the Militia, it is divided into three DISTRICTS; namely *North*, *Eaſt*, and *South* Devon; this Weſtern part being included in the laſt.

The ſubdiviſions are termed HUNDREDS; ſome of which, I underſtand, have, or lately had, their Courts;—held principally, I believe, for the recovery of debts under forty ſhillings.

HUNDRED COURTS, or Courts peculiar to the ſubdiviſions of Counties, were formerly prevalent; and might not a revival of theſe antient inqueſts, with regulations adapted to the preſent times, be rendered ſerviceable, in matters of embankment, common drains, extenſive incloſures, roads, and public nuiſances, not peculiar to any particular manor.

The MANORS of the Diſtrict are many of them ſmall; frequently, more than one being included in the ſame townſhip. The Courts are regularly held, and well attended; the rents of the lands appropriate to the manor being usually paid at the Courts.

It must not be omitted to be mentioned here, that, by the custom of this country, the inquests of manors have cognizance of the weight of bread, within their respective precincts: an admirable custom, which might well be extended.

The revival of Manor Courts, throughout the kingdom, (or the establishment of other rustic tribunals of a similar nature,) could not fail of producing the happiest effects. They are the most *natural* guardians of the rights of villagers, and the most prompt and efficient POLICE OF COUNTRY PARISHES.

I have formerly suggested the benefits which would probably arise from manorial inquests *, and the more my observations are extended, the more I am convinced of the numerous advantages which would arise from them.

The TOWNSHIPS are mostly large. Many of them have formerly been monastic.

* See YORK. ECON. Vol. I. p. 28.

naſtic. A ſufficient evidence, this, of the amenity and natural fertility of the Diſtrict.

II. The STATE OF SOCIETY. The particulars to be noticed, under this head, are

1. The towns of the Diſtrict.
2. Its villages and hamlets.
3. Its inhabitants.
4. Their habitations.
5. Their ordinary food.
6. The fuel moſt uſed.
7. The employments of working people.
8. Provident Societies.

1. The chief TOWN of the Diſtrict is *Plymouth*; which, with the new town adjoining to the dock yard, and familiarly called *Dock*, together with the village of *Stonehouſe*, which now nearly unites the new and the old towns, may be ſaid to form, at once, the PORT and the MARKET of the Diſtrict.

Taviſtock, however, in point of ſituation, and heretofore, perhaps, in that of reſpectability, might rank high among the market towns of the kingdom. It is situated in the Northern quarter of the District, among its richest lands (though beset with wild mountain scenery), and was formerly famous for its monastery. At present, though meanly built, it is a tolerable market town; and is the only inland town, in the District, now immediately under survey.

2. The VILLAGES of West Devonshire are few and small; farm houses, and many cottages, being happily scattered over the areas of the townships. Nevertheless, near most of the churches, groups of houses occur; with here and there A HAMLET.

Within one of its townships, are found the remains of a BOROUGH—*Beer-Alston*: in which, however, not a single voter, at present, resides.

3. INHABITANTS. Those of Plymouth and its environs are not objects of this survey. They have been drawn together, by war and commerce, from various quarters.

The

The natives of Devonſhire are moſtly of good perſon; tall, ſtraight, and well featured. Many of the women are of elegant figure.

In the habitudes and manners of the middle claſs, we find little which marks the inhabitants of this Weſtern extremity of the Iſland, from thoſe of the more central parts of it; except ſuch provincial diſtinguiſhments as are obſervable in almoſt every Diſtrict; and except what ariſes from an over-rated eſtimate of themſelves.

This endemial habitude, which is not obvious to ſtrangers only, but which the Gentlemen of the country, who mix with the world, are the firſt to remark, may perhaps be accounted for, without bringing any violent charge of perſonal vanity, or want of natural ſagacity, againſt the preſent inhabitants.

The coaſt of the Engliſh Channel, eſpecially its more Weſtern part, was, in much probability, the firſt part of the Iſland which was reſorted to by civilized Foreigners; and its inhabitants, of courſe, took the lead in the early ſtages of civilization in England;

land; and were far advanced, perhaps, in urbanity and useful knowledge, while the inhabitants of the more central and Northern Districts remained in a state of barbarity and ignorance. Hence, in those days, they not only felt, but really possessed, a well grounded superiority.

But, through a series of subsequent circumstances, which it would not be difficult to trace, the inhabitants of the body of the Island have long since gained the lead, in what relates to the useful arts, and modern improvements: a fact of which the mere Provincialists of this extremity of it do not appear to be yet sufficiently apprized; or, somewhat unfortunately for their country, cannot yet allow themselves to acknowledge.

I endeavour to place this circumstance, in what appears to me its just light, the rather, as it has tended, more than any other, perhaps, to prevent the country from profiting by modern discoveries.

Indeed, of late years, the SPIRIT OF IMPROVEMENT has not slumbered more composedly, in the Highlands of Scotland, than

than it has in this part of England: and with reſpect to civilization and moral conduct, among the lower claſſes of ſociety, the Highlanders are very far ſuperior to the Miners and Mountaineers of Cornwall and Devonſhire. A ſpirit of riot and outrage may be ſaid to diſtinguiſh them from the other inhabitants of the Iſland.

4. The HABITATIONS of the Diſtrict, immediately under notice, are ſuperior to thoſe of moſt other parts of the Iſland; owing chiefly, perhaps, to the MATERIALS of BUILDING being plentiful and good. *Stone* is almoſt everywhere abundant; and *ſlates* of the firſt quality for covering are procurable at a ſmall expence; and *lime* for cement is alſo a cheap article. Even the cottages are moſtly comfortable, and ſometimes neat. The farm buildings are generally ſubſtantial and commodious, compared with thoſe of many Diſtricts, for farms of ſimilar ſize.

5. The FOOD of working people is ſomewhat below par. *Barley bread*, *ſkim-milk cheeſe*, and *potatoes*, are principal articles of food, among laborers and ſmall working

working farmers. Formerly, barley bread was prevalent at the tables of the middle classes of society. The beverage is chiefly *cider*; or, during a scarcity of this, *beer*: the liquors are a base kind of spirit drawn from the lees of cider, and smuggled French brandy.

6. The FUEL of farmers and cottagers, in the inclosed country, is invariably *wood*; on the skirts of the mountains, *peat*, or *turf*, is in use. Lime is burnt chiefly or wholly with Welch *culm*, and Plymouth has a supply of Newcastle *coals*.

7. The EMPLOYMENTS of the District are chiefly those of *husbandry*. The little *mining* which has lately been done, has been carried on chiefly, I believe, with miners from the Western parts of Cornwall. At Tavistock, is a *Serge manufactory*, but not, I believe, of any great extent, and the *spinning of worsted* employs, of course, some of the female villagers in its neighbourhood. Much worsted yarn, however, is sent out of Cornwall, to be woven in Devonshire; where *women* are employed in the *weaving of serges*.

8. PRO-

8. PROVIDENT SOCIETIES, or BOX CLUBS. Theſe valuable inſtitutions were introduced into this Diſtrict, about thirty years ago. In Taviſtock and its neighbourhood, there is one or more, I underſtand, for *ſingle women* (moſtly ſerge weavers); and ſome of the Men Clubs, I am told, make a proviſion for *widows*.

The encouragement of theſe Clubs is a National object of the firſt magnitude. Not more with a view to leſſen the preſent heavy burdens of the poor, than to inſtil, into the lower claſſes of ſociety, a principle of frugality, and a ſenſe of ſocial duties, which theſe Meetings, under ſuitable regulations, cannot fail of producing.

III. PUBLIC WORKS. The natural abruptneſs of the country renders public EMBANKMENTS, and DRAINS, unneceſſary; and INLAND NAVIGATIONS difficult. So far as the tide carries up the veſſels, ſo far navigation goes; but no farther, at preſent. Nevertheleſs, a navigable communication between the two ſeas is moſt deſirable; as will be ſhewn in the courſe of theſe Volumes.

The

The "LEAT," or MADE BROOK, which ſupplies Plymouth with water, is one of the moſt uſeful and ſtriking works of the Diſtrict. An account of it will appear in the MINUTES.

PUBLIC CORN MILLS are uſually ſupplied with water, by means of ſimilar leats.

Theſe moſt antient of public works ſtill remain, here, in their priſtine ſtate. The poor take their own corn to the mill, and there dreſs it, themſelves; the miller finding them dreſſing ſieves; and the farmer of whom it is purchaſed, a horſe, to take it and the female who dreſſes it, to the mill. Cuſtoms which mark very ſtrongly the ſimplicity of manners, that ſtill prevails, in this remote part of the Iſland.

"PASSAGES," or PUBLIC FERRIES, acroſs the eſtuaries, are numerous.

The BRIDGES are few, and, in general, mean.

The ROADS of Weſt Devonſhire are, at preſent, moſt remarkable for their ſteepneſs. Leſs than half a century ago, they were mere gullies, worn by torrents in the rocks; which appeared in ſteps, as ſtaircaſes,

cases, with fragments lying loose in the indentures. Speaking with little if any latitude, there was not, then, a wheel carriage in the District; nor, fortunately for the necks of travellers, any horses but those which were natives of the country.

At length, however, good turnpike roads are formed, between town and town, throughout this quarter of the Island; and most of the villages have carriage roads opened to them; though many of these by roads, as yet, are narrow, and abound with steeps. In Devonshire, as in other mountainous countries, the first inhabitants crossed the hills, on foot, in straight forward paths. When horses came into use, the same tracks were pursued; and some of them have been continued, in use, to the present time.

INCLOSURES. This District has no traces of common fields. The cultivated lands are all inclosed; mostly in well sized inclosures; generally large in proportion to the sizes of farms.

They have every appearance of having been formed from a state of common pasture;

ture; in which ſtate, ſome conſiderable part of the Diſtrict ſtill remains; and what is obſervable, the better parts of thoſe open commons have evidently heretofore been in a ſtate of aration; lying in obvious ridges and furrows; with generally the remains of hedgebanks, correſponding with the ridges; and with faint traces of buildings.

From theſe circumſtances, it is underſtood, by ſome men of obſervation, that theſe lands have formerly been in a ſtate of permanent incloſure, and have been thrown up again, to a ſtate of commonage, through a decreaſe in the population of the country.

But from obſervations, made in different parts of Devonſhire, theſe appearances, which are common, perhaps, to every part of the county, would rather ſeem to have ariſen out of a cuſtom, peculiar perhaps to this part of the Iſland, and which ſtill remains in uſe, of lords of manors having the privilege of letting portions of the common lands, lying within their reſpective precincts, to tenants, for the purpoſe of taking one or more crops of corn, and then ſuffering

fering the land to revert to a ſtate of graſs and commonage.

In the infancy of ſociety, and while the country remained in the foreſt ſtate, this was a moſt rational and eligible way of proceeding. The rough ſides of the dells and dingles, with which it abounds, were moſt fit for the production of wood; the flatter better parts of the ſurface of the country were required for corn and paſturage; and how could a more ready way of procuring both have been fallen upon, than that of giving due portions of it to the induſtrious part of the inhabitants, to clear away the wood, and adjuſt the ſurface; and, after having reaped a few crops of corn, to pay the expence of cultivation, to throw it up to graſs, before it had been too much exhauſted to prevent its becoming, in a few years, profitable ſward? In this manner, the country would be ſupplied progreſſively, as population increaſed, with corn and paſturage, and the foreſts be converted, by degrees, into common paſtures, or HAMS.

 The

The wild or unreclaimed lands being at length gone over in this way, ſome other ſource of arable crops would be requiſite. Indeed, before this could take place, the paſture grounds would be diſproportionate to the corn lands: and out of theſe circumſtances, it is highly probable, roſe the preſent INCLOSURES.

IV. PRESENT PRODUCTIONS.

In regiſtering the preſent produce of the Diſtrict, we will obſerve the ſame order, in which its natural characters were reviewed; and enumerate,

1. The products of its waters.
2. The produce of its ſoils.
3. The productions of its ſubſtrata.

1. Of its WATERS. The ſea, which waſhes the Southern ſkirts of the Diſtrict, is ſingularly productive. The market of Plymouth has long, I believe, been eſteemed the firſt in the Iſland, for the abundance, variety, and excellency of its SEA FISH. Of late years, however, this market

market has been the worſe ſupplied, as the prime fiſh, caught by the fiſhermen in its vicinity, have been contracted for, by dealers, for that of Bath. And ſome ſhare of the finny treaſure, which theſe ſhores produce, is ſent, I underſtand, to the London market.

In a political view, however, the PILCHARD FISHERY of Cornwall is the moſt worthy of attention. In ſome ſeaſons, the quantities that are ſaid to be caught are almoſt incredible; employing many veſſels and men in taking and curing them; and affording an article of foreign traffic, of no mean conſideration.

The produce of the rivers of the Diſtrict is chiefly SALMON: which reſort to them, in great abundance; though not in ſuch numbers, as they do to ſome of the rivers, in the Northern parts of the Iſland.

There is a remarkable circumſtance regularly takes place, with reſpect to the time at which Salmon enter the two rivers ---the Tamer and the Tavey. They uſually begin to go up the latter, in the month of February; but are not found in the former, until ſome two months or more afterward; and this notwithſtanding the diſtance of their junction from the ſea; and notwithſtanding the Tamer is the larger river.

The natural hiſtory, and habits, of this moſt valuable of river fiſh, is a ſubject of enquiry, not unworthy of public attention. Beſide throwing into the market a conſiderable ſupply of human food, this ſpecies of produce brings in an income to individuals of many thouſand pounds a year: public and private advantages, which might, in much probability, be doubled, by judicious regulations and laws, reſpecting the preſervation and encouragement of this ſource of national produce; which occupies no part of the lands, nor conſumes any part of the produce of the ſoil; furniſhes a conſiderable increaſe of nutriment, without incurring any counter diminution; and is obtained at little expence of labor or attention.

It is a practice, in every Diſtrict of the Iſland, perhaps, for the diſſolute part of thoſe who live near the ſources of rivers, to to take Salmon in the act of spawning: a crime for which scarcely any punishment can be too severe. In destroying one, at this juncture of time, the existence of hundreds, perhaps thousands, may be prevented.

Some particulars, relating to this article of produce, will appear in the following MINUTES.

2. The present produce of the SOIL is in a considerable proportion, WOOD; which fills the dells and narrow vallies; and hangs on the rugged sides of more insulated hills; and which grows in great abundance, upon the extraordinary fence mounds, which will be hereafter described.

The rough open pasture grounds bear little wood, strictly speaking. But the DWARF FURZE *, and the HEATHS, occupy

* The DWARF TRAILING FURZE. This plant is common to the more Western and Southern Counties. Its appearances and habits are so perfectly different from those of the ordinary species of Furze, and it preserves those distinguishing characters so perfectly pure and permanent, when intermixed as it frequently is with the tall upright species, that they may well be considered as distinct plants.

occupy no ſmall portion of their ſurfaces.

Of the incloſed lands, in a ſtate of Agriculture, a large proportion is GRASS—perhaps two thirds of the whole. The reſt is occupied by ARABLE CROPS, and ORCHARD GROUNDS.

The ANIMAL PRODUCTIONS of the Diſtrict are the ordinary domeſtic animals of the reſt of the kingdom.

Viewing theſe ſeveral productions of the ſoils of this Diſtrict, in a political light, we find them to exceed its conſumption; and to afford ſome ſupply to the national demands. A conſiderable portion of the wood goes to the ſupply of the King's ſhips, brewery, and bakehouſes, at Plymouth. Much barley is, I underſtand, ſome years, ſent out of the Diſtrict; and numbers of cattle, every year, travel Eaſtward, on their way to the markets of the metropolis; by the route which will hereafter be deſcribed; and, of ſheep, ſome few may be drawn towards the ſame center. Beſide, it is obſervable, that, of the ſheep, ſwine, poultry, and a variety of vegetable productions which find a market within the

the Diſtrict, much goes to the ſupply of the dock yards and ſhips of war. We muſt not, however, omit to remark, at the ſame time, that the population of the Diſtrict itſelf is much below par. The inhabitants, which it at preſent contains, are chiefly employed in raiſing the productions of which we have here ſpoken.

3. The products of the SUBSTRATA have been enumerated; as STONES, SLATES, TIN, LEAD, SILVER, COPPER. Yet, notwithſtanding the natural treaſures with which the Diſtrict has abounded*, and which has been drawn from its bowels, during a ſucceſſion of ages, we do not find it either richer or happier, than other Diſtricts of the Iſland, to which Nature has been leſs bountiful of ſubter-

* Formerly, *this* Diſtrict was the principal ſcene of MINING: but, of later years, little had been done; until very lately; when the advanced price of tin induced the adventurous to re-open ſome of the old mines, and to try their luck in new ones: to the annoyance of the country; and with little profit to themſelves.

The MINES, which are worked at preſent, are chiefly in the Weſtern parts of Cornwall.

ranean wealth. On the contrary, we here find civilization, and the arts, in the rear.

This, perhaps, is a natural and inevitable conſequence of mining; which not only immerſes the lower claſs in the moſt abject employment, and buries them in the depths of ignorance; but, by exciting a ſpirit of adventure and ſpeculation in the middle and upper claſſes, draws off their attention from the more regular and certain advantages, which accrue from agriculture, manufacture, and the other uſeful arts of life.

Viewing the ſubject in this light, it appears to be ſound policy in the CHINESE GOVERNMENT, to ſuppreſs mining, and to direct the induſtry of its myriads of ſubjects to THE CULTURE OF THE SOIL, AND THE MANUFACTURE OF ITS PRODUCE.

V. THE FACE OF THE COUNTRY. The infinite variety of ſurface which this Diſtrict affords, the irregularly winding eſtuaries, and the rapid torrents, by which it is interſected, and the wild coppices that hang on the ſides of its hills, down perhaps to the immediate margins of the rivers and eſtuaries,

eſtuaries, exhibit ſcenery the moſt romantic and pictureſque. But the views generally want lawn to give them ſoftneſs and beauty. When the meadows of Buckland, and the meek grounds of Mariſtow, blend their lawny ſurfaces with the wood and water, ſcenes the moſt delightful are formed.

The broader views that frequently preſent themſelves are not leſs intereſting. The grandeur of the diſtant mountains of Dartmore and Cornwall would give effect to leſs picturable foregrounds. Plymouth Sound, partially hid by Mountedgecumbe (a prominent and ſtriking feature ſeen from every knoll), form another charming diſtance. A globular hillock, ſeated on the Eaſtern banks of the eſtuary of the Tamer, below the church of St. Budix, commands a circle of views, equal in richneſs and variety of viſual effect, to any other this Iſland poſſeſſes. To the Eaſt, the church of St. Budix, with the ſweetly wooded ſcenery of Tamerton Foliot, backed by the ſavage "Tors" of Dartmore. To the Weſt, the eſtuary of St Germains, lying as a lake, a lake, among the cultivated rising grounds of Cornwall. To the North, the estuaries of the Tamer and the Tavey, terminated with bold broken woody heights, and backed by the Cornish mountains. To the South, the lower part of the same estuary, including Hamoze, with the ships of war in ordinary; the church of Plymouth and the prominent features around it; the Sound, with ships under sail, skreened on the left with the cultivated hills of South Devonshire, on the right by Mountedgecumbe. A more interesting subject for a Panorama painting could not well be conceived.

SECTION

SECTION THE THIRD.

THE PRESENT STATE OF THE DISTRICT AS PRIVATE PROPERTY.

THE SPECIES of property attached to land ſeparates, in this as in other Diſtricts, into two orders: namely,

I. Poſſeſſory property in the land itſelf.
II. Abſtract rights ariſing out of it.

I. POSSESSORY RIGHT, or LANDED PROPERTY, puts on an appearance, here, very different from that which it wears in other parts of the kingdom. The feeſimple is principally in the poſſeſſion of men of large property. But inſtead of *letting* out their lands to tenants, at an annual rent equivalent to their value, they are

are *ſold*, in ſmall parcels or farms, generally for THREE LIVES named by the purchaſer, or ninetynine years, provided any one of the parties, named, ſurvives that period: reſerving, however, a ſmall annual rent, together with a heriot or other forfeiture, on the death of each nominee, ſimilar to thoſe attached to the copyhold tenure; which this ſpecies of tenancy, *or* tenure, very much reſembles: it being uſual to put in freſh lives, as the preceding ones drop off; receiving a fine or adequate purchaſe, for the addition of a freſh life, or lives.

This ſtate of landed property, which is common to the WEST OF ENGLAND, forms one of the many ſtriking features, which Rural Economy at preſent exhibits, in this part of the Iſland.

The advantages of this ſtate of landed property are few; its diſadvantages many. It is a ſatisfaction to the purchaſer to know, that, during his own life, and perhaps during that of his ſon, the land whoſe temporary poſſeſſion he has thus purchaſed will remain in his family; and theory ſuggeſts that, with ſuch a hold, the improvement and

and enriching of *his own eſtate*---for as ſuch it is ever eſtimated---muſt of courſe become the great object of his life. But unfortunately for himſelf and his family, as well as for the community, he has laid out his whole on the purchaſe, and has not a ſhilling left for improvements: nay, has perhaps borrowed part of the purchaſe money; and has thus entailed on himſelf and his family lives of poverty and hard labor. Whereas, had he expended the ſame money, in ſtocking and improving a rented farm, he might have enriched his family, and have thrown into the markets a much greater proportionate quantity of produce. Beſide, the poſſeſſion depends, perhaps, on his own life, and he has a wife and a young family of children. He dies, and of courſe leaves them deſtitute: while, to add to their misfortunes, the bailiff of the manor, in the hour of their diſtreſs, deprives them, perhaps, of the beſt part of the pittance he has left them.

Another evil tendency of life leaſes is that of exciting a ſpirit of ſpeculation and gambling, and of alienating the minds of men

men from the plain and more certain path of induſtry. Purchaſing a life leaſe is putting in a ſtake at a game of chance. An inſtance fell within my own knowledge, in which two ſets of lives have ceaſed, and of courſe the eſtate has been twice ſold, while a woman who was excluded, through a *mere circumſtance*, from being one of the nominees in the firſt purchaſe, is ſtill living. And, on the other hand, there is a well known inſtance, in which the leſſee, at the expiration of the term of ninetynine years, tendered his leaſe, in perſon, to the deſcendant of him, from whom his anceſtor had received it.

To the proprietor of an eſtate, this is, in many reſpects, a diſagreeable ſpecies of tenancy. His income, as has been ſhewn, is exceedingly uncertain; and, what to a man of ſentiment is worſe, it literally ariſes out of the deaths and diſtreſſes of the inhabitants of his eſtate: beſide the unpleaſant and unprofitable circumſtance of having his lands in everlaſting bondage. Let them lie aukwardly for the tenants, or intermixed with the lands of others, or in

farms

farms of improper ſizes, he has no opportunity of adjuſting or altering them. He can have no *hope* of two or three adjoining tenants dying at the ſame time. Nothing leſs than the plague, peſtilence, or famine, can aſſiſt him in a meaſure ſo ſalutary, both for himſelf and the community.

Theſe diſagreeable circumſtances have induced ſeveral men of property, to ſuffer the life leaſes of their eſtates to drop in; and, afterwards, to let their lands for an annual rent, agreeably to the practice of the reſt of the kingdom.

This deſirable change, however, can only be effected by men whoſe incomes are not wholly dependant on this ſpecies of property. Neverthele ſs, any man who is poſſeſſed of ſuch property, and is not in diſtreſſed circumſtances, may releaſe the ſmaller farms from this unprofitable and impolitic ſtate; and, in the courſe of two or three generations, the whole might be ſet at liberty, without ſenſible inconvenience to the proprietors.

It is obſervable, however, that there is ſome-

ſometimes an inconveniency ariſes to a proprietor of life leaſes, in ſuffering his farms to drop into hand ; eſpecially when the laſt life happens to linger. In this caſe, the land is exhauſted, and the premiſes ſtripped : for the property changes with the laſt breath of the dying nominee.

But, fortunately for both parties, there is an effectual mode of preventing this evil; namely, by granting the leſſee, or his repreſentative, a reſtrictive leaſe, for a term of three or more years, to commence on the death of the laſt nominee : a liberal and wiſe regulation, which ſome few men make, and which common prudence requires. The intereſts of the landlord, the tenant, and the public, are thereby jointly benefited.

II. ABSTRACT RIGHTS. Of the numerous claims to which the lands of this realm are liable, three only will be noticed, here : namely,

1. Manorial rights
2. Tithes.
3. Poor's rate.

1. MA-

1. MANORIAL RIGHTS. There are two ſpécies of property attached to the manors of this Diſtrict, which belong not to Engliſh manors in general. Theſe are mines and fiſheries.

The profit ariſing from MINES is either a ſum certain, paid by the miner to the lord of the ſoil, for ſuffering him to break, encumber, and for ever deſtroy it; or ſome certain proportion of the mineral produced; as every fifth, tenth, or twentieth "diſh."

Of the SALMON FISHERY of the Diſtrict, ſome accounts will appear in the MINUTES.

2. TITHES. It is, I believe, the univerſal practice, in the Diſtrict under ſurvey, for the Rector, whether lay or clerical, to ſend valuers over his pariſh preſently before harveſt, to eſtimate the value of his tithes. If the owner of the crop approves of the valuation, he reaps the whole of it: if not, the Rector gathers his tithe in kind: a circumſtance, however, which, I underſtand, ſeldom takes place.

This mode of ſettlement is certainly

 more

more eligible, for all parties, with respect to the existing crop, than that of collecting tithes in kind. But, with respect to the discouragement of improvements in Agriculture, they are precisely equivalent.

3. POOR'S RATE. It is worthy of remark, that, notwithstanding the wages of the country are low, as will hereafter appear, the parish rates are moderate. In Buckland, and the contiguous parishes, the poor's rate, on a par, is not more than two shillings in the pound, rack rent.

This fact, perhaps, may be the best accounted for, in the circumstance of the wool, which the country produces, being manufactured within it: not, however, in public manufactories, by the dissolute of every age and sex, drawn together from all quarters, as if for the purpose of promoting dissoluteness, debility, and wretchedness: but in private families; by men, women, and children, who, by this employment, are kept at their own houses, are enured to habits of industry, are enabled to support themselves, at all seasons, and are always at hand, to assist in the works of husbandry,

bandry, whenever the production, or the preservation, of the necessaries of life requires their assistance.

Manufactures carried on, in this rational manner, are highly beneficial to a country: while those which are prosecuted by detached bodies of people, in towns, or populous manufactories, may be considered as one of the greatest evils any country can be afflicted with.

Many substantial reasons might be adduced to shew, that AGRICULTURE AND MANUFACTURE SHOULD GO HAND IN HAND.

THE

RURAL ECONOMY

OF

WEST DEVONSHIRE;

AND THE

EASTERN PARTS OF CORNWALL.

RURAL ECONOMICS comprise three subjects, distinct in their more essential parts, but closely connected in their ramifications, which blend, in such a manner, as to unite the whole in one connected subject, and form the most useful branch of human knowledge.

The HUMAN SPECIES receive their subsistence from the soil,—are, in reality, themselves a produce of it. In the more advanced states of population, their existence may be said to rest on the right application and management of the lands, they collectively hold in possession.

LANDED POSSESSIONS, in a ſtate of accumulation, become too extenſive to be profitably occupied by individual poſſeſſors; who, therefore, parcel out their reſpective lands, among a plurality of occupiers, to whom a ſpecies of temporary poſſeſſion is given, and they, in return, give a ſuitable conſideration for ſuch temporary occupancy.

But before a LANDED ESTATE can be diſpoſed of, in this manner, with due propriety, it is neceſſary to aſſign the lands it contains to their proper uſes: as to ſeparate thoſe which produce, and are fit for producing *wood*, from thoſe which are adapted to the purpoſes of *Agriculture*; and, this done, to ſeparate the latter into ſuitable parcels, or *farms*; agreeably to their reſpective ſoils and ſituations. The farms thus laid out require *buildings*, *fences*, *roads*, *&c. &c.* ſuitably adapted to each. Theſe arrangements and operations, added to the appreciation of the ſeveral parcels, the choice of proper perſons to occupy them, the regulations and reſtrictions neceſſary to be underſtood by the parties, together

together with the unremitting care and ſuperintendance, which an extenſive eſtate and its occupiers require, form a ſeparate and very important branch of Rural Management.

Again,—WOODLANDS, which were formerly committed to the care of farm occupiers, who reaped the undergrowth, as a produce of their holds, the timber being reſerved for the owners of the lands, are now generally, and very properly, detached from tenanted lands, and placed under the care and ſuperintendance of woodwards, acting as aſſiſtants to the managers of eſtates; the whole produce, whether of timber or undergrowth, being reaped by the proprietor of the ſoil.

This MANAGEMENT of GROWN WOODS, is in itſelf an employment of ſome conſideration, and, when united with the propagation of woodlands, whether by PLANTING or by SEMINAL CULTIVATION, forms the ſecond ſubject of Rural Economy.

The laſt is AGRICULTURE; or the cultivation of farm lands; whether in the occupation of proprietors, or their tenants: a ſubject, which, viewed in all its branches, and to their fulleſt extent, is not only the moſt important, and the moſt difficult, in Rural Economics, but in the circle of human Arts and Sciences.

From this analyſis it appears, that RURAL ECONOMY comprizes three ſeparable ſubjects; namely,

First, Tenanted eſtates, and their management.

Second, The production and management of woodlands.

Third, Agriculture, or the management of farm lands.

Neverthelеſs, viewed in the ſyntheſis, they form a diſtinct branch of knowledge, with which it is incumbent on every man whoſe fortune is veſted in landed property, to be familiarly converſant.

DIVISION THE FIRST.

LANDED ESTATES,

AND THEIR

MANAGEMENT,

IN

WEST DEVONSHIRE, &c.

I.

ESTATES.

THE SPECIES of landed property, that prevails in this Diſtrict, has been noticed.

The SIZES OF ESTATES are various. There are a few of conſiderable extent.

The PROPRIETORS are the DUKE OF BEDFORD, who has a large eſtate lying round Taviſtock; the EARL of MOUNT-EDGECUMBE has now a conſiderable property, on both ſides of the Tamer. The DRAKE

DRAKE ESTATE, now LORD HEATHFIELD'S, is extenſive. Mr. HEYWOOD has a good property in the Diſtrict. Mr. RATCLIFFE, Mr. ELFORD, and other ſmaller proprietors, are in poſſeſſion, or have the ſuperiority, of the remainder.

2.

THE MANAGEMENT OF LANDED ESTATES.

IN a Diſtrict where landed property is clogged with ſo cumbrous a burden as that of life leaſes, a general ſuperiority of management cannot with reaſon be expected: nevertheleſs, it will be proper to examine the preſent practice of the Diſtrict; which is not wholly under that encumbrance: beſide, it is often as ſerviceable to the practitioner, to expoſe defects, as it is to point out excellencies of practice.

The DIVISIONS of this ſubject, which require to be examined, on the preſent occaſion, are,

I. Lay-

I. Laying out eſtates into woodlands and farm lands.

II. Laying out farm lands into diſtinct tenements or farms.

III. Farm buildings, &c.

IV. Fences.

V. Diſpoſal of farms.

VI. Forms of leaſes.

VII. Rental value of land.

VIII. Time of entry and removal.

IX. Manor Courts, and the receipt of rents.

I. LAYING OUT ESTATES. In the diſtribution of lands to their proper uſes, as into WOODLANDS and FARMS, little perhaps has been done, ſince the original laying out of TOWNSHIPS, in the manner already ſuggeſted. The ſteep ſides of the hills have been ſuffered to remain in wood, the flatter, and more eaſily culturable parts, being converted to the purpoſes of huſbandry. This, however, is not, at preſent, invariably the caſe: the tops, as well as the ſides, of ſome of the ſwells,

ſwells, are ſtill occupied by wood; and though it may frequently happen that, where this is the caſe, the land is equally as well adapted to that ſpecies of produce, as to cultivation; yet this is not always the caſe: and ſomething, though not much perhaps, ſtill remains to be done in this department of management.

II. LAYING OUT FARM LANDS. In the diſtribution of culturable lands, into diſtinct holdings, the Diſtrict under view may claim ſome merit. The farms, though of different ſizes, are many of them ſmall; perhaps too many of them are of this deſcription; but, in general, they lie well about the homeſtall; or rather, we ſhould ſay, the homeſteads have been judiciouſly placed within the areas of the lands; not in villages; as is too often the caſe, in many parts of the Iſland.

III. FARMERIES. The SITUATIONS of homeſteads, or farm buildings and yards, are generally well choſen; as the ſide of a valley, or near the head of a coomb or or dell. A ſuitable ſhelter, and a rill of water, appear to have been principal objects, in the choice of farmſteads.

In ſituations deſtitute of natural rills, "LEATS," or made rills, are cut, and have been time immemorial employed, in bringing what is called, in the pure language of ſimplicity, "potwater"— to farm houſes, and hamlets of cottages, in upland ſituations: an admirable expedient, which is applicable in many parts of the Iſland: yet which, until of late years, in Yorkſhire *, has never been practiſed perhaps out of this extreme part of the Iſland. How ſlow has hitherto been the progreſs of rural improvements!

The PLANS OF FARMERIES, here, have nothing to engage particular attention. The barns are ſmall; and the cattle yards furniſhed moſtly with open ſheds—prov. "linhays," with troughs or mangers in the back parts, to hold fodder.

Sometimes theſe linhays are double: the ſame ſpan roof furniſhing two ranges of ſheds,

* See YORK. ECON. Vol. I. page 174.

ſheds, and ſerving two yards, ſeparated by a fence partition, running along the middle of it. A ſpecies of farm building, which might be adopted in many caſes. Theſe open ſheds are uſed for cows, and young cattle; oxen being generally kept in houſes or hovels, provincially "ſhippens," during the winter.

The MATERIALS of FARM BUILDINGS are chiefly *ſtone*; moſtly the light blue ſlate ſtone, which has been deſcribed. For farm offices, earthen walls—prov. "*cobb walls*," are common.

Indeed, in ſituations, where ſtone is not at hand, "cobb" is a common material of farm buildings, throughout the WEST OF ENGLAND. Not only houſes and offices, but yard walls, and even garden walls, are commonly built with it; and endure for a length of time; provided they are kept dry. Single walls are coped; generally with thatch.

In building theſe walls, ſtraw is mixed with the earth, in a ſtate of paſte, and incorporated with it, by treading or otherwiſe, in a way ſimilar to that uſed in making the clay-

clay floors of Norfolk *. The walls are carried up, in courſes of eighteen inches, to two feet high, and fourteen inches to two feet thick; the preceding courſe being ſuffered to ſtiffen, before the ſucceeding one be ſet on. I have ſeen, in different parts of the Weſt of England, cottages two ſtories high, with no other ſupport for the joiſts and timbers, than theſe earthen walls.

In ſituations expoſed to Weſterly winds, the walls of dwelling houſes of every material are frequently guarded with *ſlates*, put on ſcale-wiſe, as upon roofs, to prevent the "ſea air" from penetrating the walls, and giving dampneſs to the rooms. In towns, the ſhells of houſes are not uncommonly built of *wood*; lathed; plaiſtered; and ſlated.

Houſes fronted with well coloured ſlate, put on neatly, and with "black mortar" (namely cement, among which pounded forge cinders have been freely mixed), are not unſightly. But ſmeared, in ſtripes or patches,

* See NORFOLK ECON. Vol. II. Page 24.

patches, with white mortar, ouzing out of the joints, and ſpreading partially over the ſurface, the appearance is filthy.

In the uſe of *rough-caſt*, or "ſlap-daſh," the Devonſhire workmen are proficient. They render it pleaſing to the eye and durable. It is ſometimes formed with a ſpecies of ſhining gravel, found upon the moorlands, which gives it, when the ſun ſhines upon it, a ſplendid effect. It is uſual to draw croſs lines over the ſurface, to give it the appearance of dreſſed ſtone-work. Not only the practice, but the theory of rough-caſting is here underſtood; as will appear in the MINUTES.

The COVERING MATERIALS of the Diſtrict are *ſlate* and *thatch*—prov. "reed," namely, unbruiſed ſtraw; the grain being ſeparated from the ſtraw without breaking it; in the manner which will be hereafter deſcribed: a practice common, I believe, to the WEST OF ENGLAND. Straw thus preſerved makes a neat and durable covering; and, when no other ſpecies of covering can be procured, it is certainly preferable to thraſhed ſtraw; which, being leſs durable,

rable, tends ſtill more to the impoveriſhment of the lands that are robbed of it.

IV. FENCES. Nothing marks the rural management of this extremity of the Iſland more ſtrongly, than the CONSTRUCTION of its farm fences.

The bank or foundation of a Devonſhire "hedge" is a mound of earth, eight, ten, or more feet wide, at the baſe, and ſometimes nearly as much in height; narrowing to ſix, ſeven, or more feet wide, at the top; which is covered with coppice woods, as Oak, Aſh, Sallow, Birch, Hazel. Theſe are cut, as coppice wood, at fifteen or twenty years growth, and at more, perhaps, than twenty feet high, beſide the height of the mound; together forming a barrier, perhaps thirty feet in height.

A ſtranger, unaware of this practice, conſiders himſelf as travelling perpetually in deep hollow ways; paſſing on, for miles, perhaps, without being able to ſee out of them; though the moſt delightful ſcenery may have accompanied him.

 The

The ORIGIN of theſe extraordinary fences may not be difficult to aſſign. By clearing the foreſts, in the manner which has been ſuggeſted, the natural fuel of the country was, of courſe, materially abridged; and, where the general face of the country was tolerably level, the ſides of the vallies were too few, and inſufficiently extenſive, to ſupply this neceſſary of life. And it appears to me moſt probable, that theſe COPPICE FENCES were adopted to ſupply this defect of fuel; and they have proved, perhaps, the beſt expedient that could have been ſtruck out. Many farms have no other *woodland,* nor ſupply of fuel, than what their fences furniſh; yet are amply ſupplied with this; beſide, perhaps, an overplus of poles, cord wood, faggots, and the bark of oak, for ſale. Hedgewood is looked up to as a crop; and is profitable as ſuch; beſide the benefit received from the mounds and ſtubs, as fences.

The AGE of moſt of theſe fences is great beyond memory. Nevertheleſs, they are continued to be formed, to the preſent day.

day Indeed, it may be ſaid, there is no other method of raiſing a live fence in uſe, in the Diſtrict.

I have met with ſeveral inſtances of RAISING fences in this way. One, to which I paid ſome attention, was formed ſeven feet wide at the baſe, and about ſeven feet high; the ſides being carried up with ſods, and battered ſomewhat inward. The coſt of it, about two ſhillings a yard in length: namely, eighteen pence for labor, and ſix pence for gathering plants, in the woods, to ſet upon it. I have ſeen plants as thick as the leg, with ſtems left two or three feet high, ſet on the top of theſe mound fences: a practice, however, which is evidently improper; as not only the labor of collecting, carriage, and planting, is greater, but the probability of ſucceſs is leſs, than they would be, if younger plants were uſed.

The ADVANTAGES of coppice fences are thoſe of being an inſuperable barrier to ſtock,—of affording extraordinary ſhelter and ſhade to paſturing animals,—of giving a neceſſary ſupply of fuel, in a country where no other fuel than wood can, at preſent, be compaſſed by farmers,—and of being, with ordinary care in repairing them, everlaſting. Inſtead of mouldering away, and growing leſs as they increaſe in age, the ſwelling of the roots, the falling of leaves, and decayed boughs, and the ſhovellings of their baſes thrown upon their tops, with freſh ſods brought from a diſtance, perhaps, to make good accidental breaches, tend to increaſe, rather than to diminiſh, the mounds; ſo that the bulkineſs of ſome of the old hedges may be owing to time, rather than to the original formation.

The DISADVANTAGES of the Devonſhire hedges are their firſt coſt, and the quantity of ground they occupy, and injure, by their drip and ſhade, and by the ſoil uſed in their formation: Five and twenty feet is the leaſt that can be reckoned, for the width of waſte. The injury they do to arable crops, in preventing a free circulation of air; and their being liable to be

torn

torn down by cattle, when the adjoining field is in a ſtate of paſture, are other diſadvantages.

But every ſpecies of fence has its diſadvantages, and whether, upon the whole, that under conſideration is preferable to the ordinary live hedge of the kingdom, I will not attempt to decide. In an Upland Diſtrict, and where the fields are of a good ſize, coppice fences are more eligible, than they would be, in a low flat country, with ſmall incloſures; and much more eligible in a Diſtrict, where wood is the only fuel, than they would be in a coal country.

To the ſportſman, theſe fences are unfriendly; and, to an invading army, they would be moſt embarraſſing: an extent of country, interſected by ſuch barriers, would be, in effect, one immenſe fortification.

V. The DISPOSAL OF FARMS in this Diſtrict may be ſaid to be threefold: namely,

Selling them for lives,
Letting them for a term, and
Occupying them in huſbandry.

The laſt, namely the practice of men of fortune OCCUPYING ſome conſiderable parts of their eſtates, appears to have been, until very lately, a prevailing faſhion among the great proprietors of Devonſhire. There is an inſtance of one noble family having kept in hand fourteen or fifteen hundred acres, for ſome generations paſt; and of another family having occupied ſeven or eight hundred acres, for more than two centuries; and, in theſe two inſtances, the lands, I believe, ſtill remain in hand. But many other proprietors, finding little income ariſing from lands thus employed, and ſome one or more, it is aſſerted, having been brought into debt by their managers (I ſpeak here of farms lying at a diſtance from the principal reſidences of their owners), ſuch farms have been wiſely let or ſold, to men who have a perſonal intereſt in their management.

Theſe domains were probably kept in the occupation of their proprietors, with a view to ſet an example to the tenants of their reſpective eſtates, in the infancy of huſbandry: and the ſtate of management, in which

which we now find the Diſtrict, may have ariſen out of this circumſtance. But men of fortune appear to have abandoned, long ago, this original intention, if ſuch it were; and to have taken for granted, that their lands were in a ſtate of perfect management.

THE SELLING OF FARMS FOR THREE LIVES, nominated by the reſpective purchaſers, as it was the antient, and once perhaps the univerſal, practice of the Diſtrict, comes next under conſideration.

At preſent, one half, or two thirds of the lands of the Diſtrict, probably, are under this ſpecies of tenure, or tenancy, or hold: the remainder being occupied by proprietors, whether men of fortune or yeomanry; and by tenants, for a term certain, or from year to year.

The diſpoſal of farms for three lives is generally by what are provincially termed SURVEYS; a ſpecies of AUCTION; at which candidates bid for the priority of refuſal, rather than for the thing itſelf; a ſpecies of ſale common to every ſpecies of property. If the higheſt bidder does not reach the ſeller's price, the bidding is inconcluſive: the ſeller names his price, and the higheſt bidder has the firſt option of choice, or refuſal. If he refuſe, the next higheſt bidder takes his choice, and ſo of the reſt: a ſpecies of ſale, which is very convenient to the ſeller.

The eſtimate value of lands, for three lives, is about eighteen years purchaſe of the neat rental value, or about fourteen years purchaſe of the groſs rent and taxes, which laſt life leſſees uſually engage to pay; together with a ſmall annual rent; and generally a heriot, forfeitable on the death of each nominee, as has been mentioned.

The purchaſer has the right of transfer, and of letting the premiſes to farm, from year to year, for a term of years, or during the term of the life leaſe. Thus becoming a ſort of middle man, between the proprietor and the occupier.

The leſſee for lives keeps up the buildings, fences, gates, &c. (the proprietor finding timber,) or is liable to pay for dilapidations. All coppice wood and under-

underwood, as well as fruit trees and other trees, except Oak, Aſh, and Elm, are, entirely, or under certain regulations, at the diſpoſal of the leſſee; and cannot be cut down, by the proprietor of the land, during the demiſe.

On the expiration of a leaſe for lives, the leſſee is allowed, by cuſtom, a few days for clearing the premiſes of liveſtock, and forty days, for dead ſtock—as grain, furniture, &c. but he cannot touch a bough, or a fixture, or remove ſtraw, dung, &c. after the moment of extinction of the laſt life.

The LETTING OF FARMS, for a year, or a term of years, is ſimilar in method of diſpoſal, to that of ſelling them for lives: ſo forcible would ſeem to be the tide of cuſtom!

In *ſelling* a farm, an auction is a ſuitable medium of diſpoſal: the ſeller receives his price or ſecurity, before he delivers up poſſeſſion; and the leſſee, himſelf, being generally one of the nominees, is, in ſome meaſure, *done with*.

But

But the caſe is very different with a man, who is to pay his rent halfyearly, and to conform with a variety of covenants and regulations, which are neceſſary to the ſpecies of tenancy, now under conſideration. In this caſe, it is not more the *rent;* than the *man*, that is to be looked to, and choſen. Among candidates, at auctions, for letting farms, are generally adventurers, who want judgment, and men of deſperate fortunes, who want a temporary ſubſiſtence; and theſe men will ever be the higheſt bidders; will ever outbid men of judgment and capital; ſuch as will pay their rent, keep up their repairs, and improve the land; and ſuch as ought ever to be, and ever are, the choice of judicious managers of eſtates. There is a fair market price for farms, as for their produce; and no man is fit to be entruſted with the management of an eſtate, who cannot aſcertain the value of its lands, and who, having aſcertained this, does not prefer a man of judgment and capital, to any *nominal rent*, which ſpeculation can offer him. It

may

may be ſaid, with little latitude, that, in the end, it is equally detrimental to an eſtate, to overrent it, as it is to let it beneath its fair rental value. This is an axiom of management which is well known to every man of landed property, who has perſevered in paying attention to his own affairs; and which has coſt ſome men no ſmall ſhare of property, reſpectability, and peace of mind, to come at the knowledge of.

The practice of letting farms by auction, in this Diſtrict, is not difficult to be accounted for. It has grown in part out of the cuſtom of ſelling farms by auction, as abovementioned; and is in part owing to the circumſtance of the immediate management of eſtates being in the hands of country attornies; who are, profeſſionally, unacquainted with the value of the lands they have to let, and who have valuable intereſts in the holding of ſurveys.

Another ſingular trait, in the management of eſtates, in this Diſtrict, may be proper to be mentioned. The agent, inſtead of receiving a ſalary adequate to his ſer-

ſervices, makes an exorbitant charge, upon the tenants, for their leaſes; each eſtate having its eſtabliſhed impoſt.

This regulation is evidently founded on fallacious principles. The intereſt of the agent ought ever to be connected with that of his principal. Whereas, by the practice now under notice, as well as by that of letting farms by auction, in the manner which has been mentioned, they are eſtranged from each other. Inſtead of its being the intereſt of the agent to promote that good order, punctuality, and ſpirit of improvement, which ought to be ſolicitouſly cheriſhed on every eſtate, his beſt intereſts are connected with the beggary and ſhifting of tenants; and, of courſe, with the confuſion and eventual injury of the eſtate: and this without any adequate counter advantage. Farmers are not ſo inattentive to their own intereſts, as to omit to calculate the expence of the leaſe, while they are bargaining for the farm; and it is well known to thoſe, who are converſant in the buſineſs of letting farms, that nothing

nothing more diſguſts a good tenant, *a man who can have a farm anywhere*, than an exorbitant charge for his leaſe.

VI. FORMS OF LEASES. In the conſtruction of leaſes, it would be unreaſonable to expect to find anything ſuperiorly excellent, in a Diſtrict where the letting of farms may be conſidered as, in ſome meaſure, a modern practice. For although it muſt ever have been in uſe, between middle men and under tenants, yet it muſt ever have been a ſecondary and ſubordinate branch of the management of eſtates; and as ſuch, indeed, it ſtill remains. Beſide, the forming of leaſes, being left to men who are unacquainted with the required covenants and regulation, neceſſary for promoting the intereſt of an eſtate, is another bar to excellency of conſtruction.

The following are the HEADS OF A LEASE, under which one of the firſt farms in the country was let, a very few years ago.

LANDLORD GRANTS the uſe of the premiſes

premiſes for twentyone years, at a fixed annual rent.

LANDLORD RESERVES the privilege of holding Courts (this being a manor farm) with the uſe of a parlour, bed room, and ſtable, one day and night, for the cuſtomary fee of two ſhillings; alſo the uſual dinner and liquor, for the Court tenants, at one ſhilling each.

ALSO all mines, quarries, &c.

ALSO timber, game, &c.

ALSO the liberty of ſowing the third crop of grain with eaver (raygraſs) and clover, to be provided by the tenant.

ALSO a right of viewing the ſtate of repair of buildings, &c. and, if neceſſary repairs are not executed within two months after notice given, the landlord may execute them at the tenant's expence.

ALSO the power of re-entry on non-performance of the agreement.

TENANT AGREES to pay rent, taxes, &c.

ALSO to do all repairs; the landlord firſt putting the premiſes into tenantable condition.

ALSO

Also to do ſuit and ſervice at the Lord's Courts.

Also to lay on fifty double Wincheſter buſhels of ſtone lime, or ſeventy ſacks of ſea ſand, an acre, the firſt year of breaking up; to be mixed with mold, in a huſband-like manner.

Also to take three crops of corn, for ſuch dreſſing, and *no more!* theſe crops being Wheat, Barley, and Oats, *in ſucceſſion!* and to ſow graſs ſeeds with the laſt crop.

Also to keep up orchard grounds; the landlord firſt ſtocking them properly with trees: the tenant afterwards having the decayed trees for filling up vacancies.

Also to repair the mounds of hedges every time the wood is felled; and not to cut them under ſeven years growth; nor to cut rods, &c. but when the hedge is felled.

Also to the following

Restrictions. Not to break up meadow grounds, under the penalty of ten pounds an acre.

Also

Also not to pare and burn the ſurface of other lands, under the ſame penalty *.

Also not to grow Rape, Hemp, Flax, Woad, Weld, Madder, or POTATOES!! unleſs for the uſe of his own family.

Also not to ſell Hay, Straw, or Turneps; nor to carry manure off the premiſes.

Also not to depaſture orchard grounds with horned cattle.

Also not to fell, lop, or top, any timber tree, under the penalty of ten pounds; nor any maiden tree or ſapling, under that of five pounds.

Also not to aſſign the leaſe, without conſent, &c.

Thoſe who *bind* tenants to ſuch a baſe ſyſtem of management, as the tenant of this charming farm is bound (for eighteen years to come!) are entitled to pity, rather than to cenſure: they copy leaſes from muſty forms, left them by their predeceſſors, as they copy black letter precepts out of Jacob and Burn.

The

* This farm lies ſomewhat to the Southward of *this* Diſtrict; being within that of the South Hams.

The heads of a leaſe of a ſmaller farm, within this Diſtrict, runs thus:

Landlord agrees to repair, &c.

Tenant to lay on a hundred buſhels of lime, or one hundred and twenty ſeams (or horſeloads) of ſea ſand, mixed with one hundred and twenty ſeams of dung, an acre, on all lands broken up for Wheat after Ley or Graſs. And not to take more than a crop of Wheat, a crop of Barley, and a crop of Oats, for ſuch dreſſing; but to ſow over the Oats twelve pounds of Clover and half a buſhel of Eaver, an acre; and not to mow the Clover more than once.

Also not to cut hedges under twelve years growth; and then when the adjoining field is broken up for wheat: and to plaſh the ſides (or outer brinks of the mounds), and ſhovel out the ditches (or hollows at the foot of the bank), throwing the mold upon the mound, to encourage the growth of the hedgewood.

Also to preſerve orchards: to keep them free from horned cattle: landlord agreeing to find young trees; tenant to fetch and plant them, and to carry two

 ſeams

ſeams of dung or freſh maiden earth to ſet each plant in: being allowed the old trees for his trouble.

ALSO not to ſell Hay, Straw, &c. except "Reed" (or unthraſhed Straw).

ALSO not to aſſign over, &c. &c. &c.

VII. RENT. The rent of the larger arable farms, on which huſbandry is the principal object, is from ten ſhillings to twenty ſhillings an acre; according to the quality of the ſoil, its ſituation, and attendant circumſtances. Small farms, with a large proportion of orchard ground lying to them, pay higher rents.

VIII. REMOVAL. Ladyday is the accuſtomed time of entry and transfer.

IX. MANOR COURTS. Theſe Courts, as we have already intimated, are regularly held. Conventionary or life-leaſe tenants are conſidered in the light of copyholders; and, by the cuſtom of the country, freeholders attend Manor Courts; which, however, are principally held for the RECEIPT OF RENTS, whether conventional or predial.

DIVISION

DIVISION THE SECOND.

WOODLANDS,

THEIR

PROPAGATION AND MANAGEMENT.

I.

WOODLANDS.

1. THE SPECIES OF WOODLAND, which is moſt prevalent in this Diſtrict, is that which comes emphatically under the denomination of WOODS: namely a mixture of Timber and Underwood; the ancient law, which requires that a certain number of Timberlings ſhall be left ſtanding, in each acre of Coppice-wood cut down, being here, more or leſs complied with; though it were only that

ſuch ſtandards ſhould be taken down at the ſucceeding fall of Underwood, and others left in their ſtead. In conſequence of this evaſion there is, in effect, much Woodland in a ſtate of COPPICE. And there is ſome little in a ſtate of TIMBER, with but little Underwood.

The HEDGEROW WOOD of the Diſtrict is invariably Coppice; with ſome few Pollards growing out of the ſides, or at the baſes, of the mounds; which are probably too high and narrow to ſupport Timber Trees upon their tops,—were the tenants to ſuffer them to riſe.

II. The SPECIES OF TIMBER TREES are principally the OAK and the ASH, with ſome ELMS on the deeper better ſoils; alſo the BEECH and the SYCAMORE. But the Oak may be emphatically termed the Timber Tree of the Diſtrict.

III. The SPECIES OF COPPICE WOODS are the OAK, the BIRCH, the SALLOW, the HAZLE, the ASH, the CHESNUT, which laſt is found, in wild recluſe ſituations,

ſituations, with every *appearance* of being a native. The WILD CHERRY, too, is found in Coppices: but little or no HAWTHORN; which does not appear to be a native of the country!

IV. The HISTORY of theſe Woodlands is unknown: tradition is ſilent on the ſubject. They are, undoubtedly, the aboriginal produce of the ſoils they now occupy. They have no appearance of cultivation; except near habitations: and even, there, unleſs in a few inſtances, Planting does not appear to have been, at any time, the practice or faſhion of the Diſtrict.

V. The ELIGIBILITY of the preſent Woodlands, in their preſent ſtate, has been mentioned: ſome ſmall portion of them ought, perhaps, to be converted to Farm Lands; though, in the ordinary modes of converſion, they might not pay fo he alteration: and there are conſiderable extents of unproductive high lands, which ought to be converted to Woodland.

2.

THE PROPAGATION OF WOODLANDS.

THE SPECIES OF WOOD, proper to be raiſed on the bleak barren heights, which are here ſpoken of as being eligible to be converted into Woodlands, appear to me evident. On the ſides of vallies, ſheltered from the cutting winds of this Diſtrict, the OAK is undoubtedly the moſt eligible ſpecies of Wood. But, upon expoſed heights, the Oak, even as Coppice wood, ſhrinks from the blaſt; and, as Timber, makes no progreſs after a certain age; becoming ſtunted and moſſy. The only Oak Timber, I have obſerved in the Diſtrict, of any ſize, grows on the lower ſkirts of the hills. Whereas the BEECH flouriſhes, even as Timber, in very bleak expoſed ſituations. And, I am of opinion, that, for COPPICE WOOD, on the bleak barren heights under notice, the BEECH and the

BIRCH

BIRCH would be moſt eligible: and that, for TIMBER, in ſuch ſituations, the LARCH, alone, is eligible.

I ſpeak, however, from a general knowledge of this valuable tree, in the ſoils and ſituations in which I have ſeen it flouriſh. For it does not appear to have been tried on the bleak barren ſoils of this Diſtrict. Yet, ſeeing the extent of ſuch ſoils, which it contains, and its ſituation with reſpect to the ſhip yards of Plymouth; and ſeeing at the ſame time, with almoſt moral certainty, that the Larch, in times to come, will be a principal article of Ship building, in this iſland, it is highly probable that whoever now propagates it, will exceedingly enhance the value of his eſtate.

3.

MANAGEMENT OF WOODLANDS.

TO convey a comprehenſive idea of this department of Rural Management, in the

Diſtrict now under view, it will be prope to ſpeak ſeparately of

I. Timber.
II. Coppice wood.
III. Hedge wood.
IV. Bark.

I. THE MANAGEMENT OF TIMBER. The chief produce of Woodlands, here, being Coppice wood, rather than Timber, leſs is required to be ſaid, under this branch of management. Indeed, judging from what has fallen under my notice, reſpecting the treatment of Timber, in this Diſtrict, little more than cenſure can be fairly attached to it.

To the TRAINING of Timber, little if any attention appears to be paid. I have ſeen Oak woods irreparably injured, and for ever rendered incapable of producing large Timber, for want of timely thinnings.

And in the only inſtance of FELLING Oak Timber, on a large ſcale, which came under my obſervation, the management, or rather miſmanagement, was ſuch as ought

ought not to be ſuffered. Inſtead of clearing the ground, or of removing the underling and ſtunted or full grown trees, to make room for thoſe which were in a thriving profitable ſtate, the latter, only, were hewn down! Many of them in the moſt luxuriant ſtate of growth; throwing them, heedleſsly, among the ſtanding trees! thus adding crime to crime, and cauſing double deſtruction. Acts like theſe ſhould be puniſhable; for it is not a waſte of private property only; but, in the preſent ſtate of Ship timber, and in the immediate vicinity of a dock yard, ſuch waſte becomes a public loſs.

Enquiring into the cauſe of this outrage, I was told (and probably with truth, as nothing elſe could well account for it) that ſo many hundred trees had been ſold, at ſuch a price, the choice of them being left to the purchaſer; who had a wide extent of Woodland to range over;, and who, guided by the exorbitant price of Bark, choſe of courſe, the full topped faſt-growing trees; as affording the moſt bark and of the beſt quality.

II. MANAGE-

II. MANAGEMENT OF COPPICES.

This forming a prominent feature in the Rural Management of the Diſtrict, it requires to be treated of in detail; under the following branches.

1. Training.
2. Age of Felling.
3. Diſpoſal.
4. Mode of Cutting.
5. Mode of Converting.
6. Conſumption.

1. THE TRAINING OF COPPICE WOODS is not, I believe, attended to farther, than to keep them free from brouzing ſtock, during the firſt ſtages of their growth. However, conſidering the advanced age at which Coppice wood is cut, here, much faggot wood, and perhaps other inferior wares, might be taken out with advantage to the riſing Coppice. The Birch and the Sallow, quick growing woods, ought certainly to be checked, ſo as to prevent their overtopping and cramping the growth of the Oak. The great object in training Coppices

Coppices is to give evenneſs and fullneſs to the whole. In a diſtrict, however, where ſtakes, edders, and wicker hurdles are not in common uſe, the leſs profitable would be the thinnings of a Coppice. In the more advanced ſtages of growth, hoops are, here, a profitable article *.

2. THE AGE OF FELLING COPPICE WOOD, in the ordinary practice of the Diſtrict, is twenty years. The bark of the Oak is a principal object, eſpecially at preſent; and this does not acquire, much ſooner, a ſufficient ſubſtance and maturation of juices, to fit it properly for the uſe of the tanner. It is oftener, I believe, ſuffered to ſtand until it be more than twenty years growth, than it is felled under that age. From eighteen to twentyfive years may, perhaps, be ſet down as the ordinary limits.

3. THE

* HOOPS for Cider caſks. The principal wood is Aſh; but Cheſnut and Wild Cherry are reckoned nearly as good. The price, in the rough, about 8d. a hundred weight. The time of cutting, December and January: the time of bending, May and June. The Coopers charge is half a crown a dozen.

3. THE DISPOSAL OF COPPICE WOOD. The common medium of ſale is the ſurvey or auction: the proper vehicle of diſpoſal, in all caſes where large allotments of wood, of every kind, are to be diſpoſed of, in the groſs; provided men of property and common honeſty can be drawn together as bidders *. But, in this Diſtrict, where the bidders at ſuch ſales are, many of them, men without property or principle, public auctions become a hazardous mode of diſpoſal; as moſt men of property, in the Diſtrict, I underſtand, have experienced.

This claſs of purchaſers are chiefly working woodmen, who unite themſelves into companies or ſets, in order that they may compaſs, the better, the parcel on ſale; afterwards, ſharing it out among themſelves; and each employing aſſiſtants to take down his own ſhare.

The prices of Coppice wood, by the acre, are various; according to the age and quality; and have lately had a rapid riſe, on account of the high price of bark; and the great demand for wood, which the war

* See YORK. ECON. Vol. I, p. 241.

war has occaſioned. Formerly, (within memory) four or five pounds an acre was reckoned a good price for wood of a middle quality, and twenty years growth. Within the laſt ten years, or leſs time, ten pounds an acre was eſteemed a full price for ſuch wood. Now (1794) it is worth fifteen pounds an acre; the purchaſer paying *tithe*; which is uſually 2s. 6d. to 3s. in the pound, upon the groſs amount of ſale.

4. THE METHOD OF TAKING DOWN COPPICE WOOD, in this part of the iſland, is ſingular. The ordinary woods being cleared away, previous to the Barking ſeaſon, THE OAK IS PEELED STANDING; all the hands employed continuing to peel during the ſpring run of the Bark. When a check takes place, the woodmen employ themſelves in cutting down the peeled wood; until the midſummer run calls them again to the operation of peeling; which, indeed, may be ſaid to laſt, with little interruption, throughout the ſummer; the wood being chiefly converted into ſaleable ware, during the winter months.

This

This unuſual mode of proceeding gives a piece of Woodland, undergoing theſe operations, a ſtriking appearance to the eye of a ſtranger, travelling through the country, in the ſummer ſeaſon. The purchaſer's ſhares are marked out in ſquare patches; and theſe divided again into ſtripes of different colours: one white, with barked poles lying along upon the ſtubs! another brown,—the leaves of the early peeled poles, yet ſtanding, being already dead, and changed to this colour: a third mottled, having naked ſtems, headed with yet green leaves; while perhaps the remainder of each patch, reſerved for another year's fall, appears in its natural green.

This method of taking down Coppice wood, however, has been practiſed, time immemorial; and, where Firewood and Bark are the principal objects of produce, a more eligible method would be difficult to ſtrike out. The practice of ſuffering the peeled ſtems to remain upon the roots, in the firſt inſtance, as well as that of afterwards letting them lie upon the ſtubs, is theoretically bad. The fact however is, this

this practice, though it may have been continued for centuries, has not destroyed, nor materially injured, the woods; which, though not equal in thickness and evenness, to the Sussex and Kentish Coppices, are upon a par with those of the rest of the Island.

5. 6. THE CONVERSION AND CONSUMPTION OF COPPICE WOOD is, here, into *poles*, for uses in husbandry, as the roofs of sheds and hovels, rails, &c. &c.; *cordwood*, mostly for the use of ships of war; *faggots* of different sorts, for fuel, and for the use of the King's bake-houses, &c. at Plymouth.

The ordinary *price of cordwood*, in time of peace, is about ten shillings a cord, of 128 cubical feet (namely 4, 4, and 8) and the poles and faggots in proportion *.

III. The MANAGEMENT OF HEDGE WOOD. This department of management

* Formerly, CORDWOOD was SOLD BY WEIGHT; a practice which is not, yet, altogether obsolete. The price about 18d. a seam, or 6d. a hundred weight.

management is ſo exactly ſimilar to that of Coppice wood, that it does not require a ſeparate detail. The bruſh wood is cleared away, in early ſpring, and the Oak peeled ſtanding, in the barking ſeaſon.

IV. The MARKET FOR BARK, after the tanneries of the country are ſupplied, is Ireland; to which it has, for ſome years laſt paſt at leaſt, been ſhipped in great quantities. This appears to be a principal cauſe of the exorbitant price, which this uſeful article of manufacture has riſen to of late years; and which bids fair to reduce to a ſtate little ſhort of annihilation, the Oak timber of this iſland, fit for Ship building.

REMARK.

THE PROCESS OF TANNING is peculiarly entitled, at this time, to the attention of the CHEMIST. The bark of the Oak, it is probable, acts principally as an aſtringent, on the texture of the hide; and might, perhaps, be equalled, or excelled, by by other aſtringents, natural or prepared, if duly ſought for, and attentively applied.

To export Oak Bark, under the preſent circumſtances, muſt ſurely be a political error.

DIVISION THE THIRD.

AGRICULTURE.

THIS moſt extenſive branch of RURAL ECONOMY requires to be examined, in detail; agreeably to the plan which I have hitherto found it requiſite to purſüe, in regiſtering the practices of other Diſtricts; and conformably to the ANALYTIC TABLE OF CONTENTS, prefixed to this Volume.

I.

FARMS.

I. THE NATURAL CHARACTERS of Farms appear, in a great meaſure, in what has been ſaid of the Natural Characters

racters of the Diſtrict; and only require to be adduced, here, in order to bring them into one point of view, with the adventitious properties of Farms, at preſent obſervable, in this extreme part of the Iſland.

The CLIMATURE is very uncertain, in an agricultural point of view. In a dry ſummer, the harveſt is early, on account of the ſoutherly ſituation of the Diſtrict. But, in a moiſt ſeaſon, it is ſometimes very backward; owing to inceſſant drizzling rains, added to the coolneſs of the ſea air. See CLIMATURE, page 11.

The ſurfaces of Farms, notwithſtanding the uneven ſurface of the country at large, are leſs ſteep and difficult to work, than the Farms of many other hilly Diſtricts; owing to the circumſtance of the ſteeper ſides of vallies being chiefly appropriated to wood.

The QUALITY OF THE SOIL has been deſcribed, as being of a ſlatey nature; moſtly abounding with fragments of ſlate rock and other ſtones; and generally mixed with a portion of loam.

The QUANTITY or depth of ſoil is greater than the par of upland ſoils; varying, from five or ſix, to ten or twelve inches.

The SUBSOIL is a rubble, or broken ſlatey rock; abſorbing water to a certain and great degree; but an exceſs of wet weather ſometimes cauſes a temporary ſurcharge; during which, the ſoil, in ſome particular ſpots, becomes wet and poachy. It may be ſaid, however, in general, the ſoil and ſubſoil are abſorbent, clean, and ſound.

II. The HISTORY of Farm Lands, in this Diſtrict, has been hinted at, as having paſſed from the foreſt or unoccupied ſtate, to a ſtate of common paſture, through the medium of at leaſt a partial cultivation; and, from the ſtate of common paſturage, to the predial ſtate, in which it now appears. But theſe ſuggeſtions ariſe, principally, from the preſent appearances of the ſurface, and from the other circumſtantial evidences, mentioned above. Theſe circumſtances, collated with the different

ſurveys

ſurveys that have been made, at diſtant periods of time, might bring this matter to a greater degree of certainty, than either of them, taken ſeparately.

III. The PRESENT APPLICATION of Farm Lands. Viewing the Diſtrict at large, Farms in general are in a ſtate of MIXED CULTIVATION; comprizing *arable land*, *temporary leys*, *water meadows*, and *orchard grounds:* GRASSLAND being the more prominent characteriſtic, as will more fully appear in ſpeaking of their management.

IV. The SIZES OF FARMS are, as they ought to be, *extremely various.* BARTONS (a name which perhaps was originally given to demeſne lands, or manor farms, but which now ſeems to be applied to any *large* farm, in contradiſtinction to the more common deſcription of farms) are generally of a full ſize; as from two or three to four or five hundred acres of culturable lands. Ordinary farms run from ten to a hundred pounds a year.

General Observations.

THE humiliating ſituation in which this country is placed, at preſent (1795), through a miſguided attachment to SPECULATIVE COMMERCE, and thro a neglect, not leſs to be lamented, of the PERMANENT INTERESTS of the country,—has given us an opportunity of ſeeing the utility which ariſes from a GRADATION OF FARMS; and from having farmers of different degrees and conditions, to furniſh the markets with a regular ſupply of grain.

Were the whole of the cultivated lands of the Iſland in the hands of ſmall needy farmers, unable to keep back the produce from the autumn and winter markets, it is highly probable that the country, during the paſt ſummer, would have experienced a ſcarcity, nearly equal to a famine; and would, every year, be at the mercy of dealers or middlemen, during the ſpring and ſummer months.

On

On the contrary, were the whole in the hands of men of large capitals, a greater ſcarcity might be experienced, in autumn and the early part of winter, than there is under the preſent diſtribution of farm lands.

I do not mean to convey, that the preſent diſtribution of farm lands is perfect, or preciſely what it ought to be, in a political point of view. Nevertheleſs, it might be highly improper, in Government, to interfere in the diſpoſal of private property. It is therefore to the conſideration of proprietors of eſtates I beg leave to offer the following principle of management, in the tenanting of their reſpective eſtates: namely, that of not entruſting their lands, whether they lie in large or in ſmall farms, in the hands of men who have not capital ſkill and induſtry, *taken jointly*, to cultivate them, with profit, to themſelves and the community; nor of ſuffering any man, let his capital be what it may, to hold more land, than he can perſonally ſuperintend; ſo as to pay the requiſite regard to the minutiæ of cultivation.

V. The PLANS OF FARMS have been ſpoken of as being generally judicious, in reſpect of having the farm-ſtead, or buildings, placed within the area of the lands. The fields too have been mentioned, as being well ſized; but ſometimes, perhaps, too large, or out of proportion, on the ſmaller farms; owing to the expenſiveneſs and *cloſeneſs* of the fences in uſe: and, owing, perhaps, to the ſame circumſtance, private lanes, or driftways, are in ſome caſes wanted. On the whole, however, the Diſtrict is above par, with reſpect to the plans of its farms.

GENERAL OBSERVATION. From this Analyſis of Farms, it is plain, that Weſt Devonſhire has many advantages, natural and fortuitous, as an AGRICULTURAL DISTRICT.

2.

FARMERS.

The SCALE of OCCUPIERS, in this Weſtern Diſtrict, is ſingularly extenſive; reaching

reaching from the largeſt proprietor, down to the farm ſervant, or pariſh prentice; who having, by his temperance and frugality, ſaved up a few pounds, and, by his induſtry and honeſty, eſtabliſhed a fair character, is entruſted with one of the ſmall holdings that are ſcattered in every pariſh; and who, perhaps, by perſevering in the ſame line of conduct, aſcends, ſtep after ſtep, to a farm of a higher order.

The QUALIFICATIONS of PROFESSIONAL OCCUPIERS, including ſmall proprietors, lifeleaſeholders, and tenants, will not be found, on a general view, at preſent, equivalent to the natural and adventitious advantages of the Diſtrict, nor ſuch as are likely to give effect to thoſe advantages; ſo as to raiſe the Rural Management of this extremity of the Iſland, to a par with that of leſs favored parts of it.

The PROPERTY of occupiers of this claſs is abſorbed in life leaſeholds. If a man can purchaſe a farm he will not rent one; and, in purchaſing, he incapacitates himſelf from occupying his purchaſe, properly.

perly. There are, no doubt, many exceptions to this general poſition.

Their EDUCATION is another bar to improvement. Many of them, as has been intimated, have riſen from ſervants of the loweſt claſs; and having never had an opportunity of looking beyond the limits of the immediate neighbourhood of their birth and ſervitude, follow implicitly the paths of their maſters.

Their KNOWLEDGE is of courſe confined; and

The SPIRIT of IMPROVEMENT deeply buried under an accumulation of cuſtom and prejudice.

There are, however, ſome few individuals, in the Diſtrict, who are ſtruggling to break through the thick cruſt of prepoſſeſſion, under which the country ſeems to have been long bound down. But they have not yet obtained, ſufficiently, the confidence of the lower claſs of occupiers. Their exertions, however, may convince the latter that the eſtabliſhed practice of the Diſtrict may be deviated from, without danger.

3. WORK.

3.

WORKPEOPLE.

NO inconſiderable ſhare of farm labor is done by farmers themſelves, their wives, their ſons, and their daughters. On the larger farms, however, workpeople of different deſcriptions are employed. They are either

I. Laborers,
II. Servants, or
III. Apprentices.

I. The LABORERS of the Diſtrict are below par: many of them drunken, idle fellows; and not a few of them may be ſaid to be honeſtly diſhoneſt; declaring, without reſerve, that a poor man cannot bring up a family on ſix ſhillings a week and honeſty. In addition, however, to theſe low wages, it is pretty common for farmers to let their conſtant laborers have corn, at a fixed price; and endeavour to give

give them piece-work,—to be paid ſor, by meaſurement, or in groſs.

Nevertheleſs, the wages of the Diſtrict, ſeeing the great riſe in the price of living, appears to me to be too low; and what the farmers ſave in the expence of labor, they probably loſe by pillage, and in the poor's rate. All ranks of people, FARM LABORERS ONLY EXCEPTED, have had an increaſe of income, with the increaſe of the prices of the neceſſaries of life; or, which is the ſame thing, with the decreaſe in the value or price of money. This may, in a great meaſure, account for the increaſe of the poor's rates, in country pariſhes, without bringing in the degeneracy and profligacy of the preſent race of working people, compared with the paſt; though ſome part of it, I believe, may be fairly laid to the charge of that degeneracy, which, if the taſk were not invidious, would not be difficult to account for.

II. SERVANTS. The moſt remarkable circumſtance, in the economy of farm ſervants, in this part of the Iſland, is that of of there being NO FIXED TIME OR PLACE OF HIRING them: a circumſtance which, I believe, prevails throughout the Weſt of England. They are hired either for the year, the half year, or by the week; the laſt a very unuſual method of retaining houſe or indoor farm ſervants. When a ſervant is out of place, he makes enquiries among his acquaintances, and goes round to the farm houſes, to offer himſelf.

In the RURAL ECONOMY of the MIDLAND COUNTIES, I made ſome obſervations on this ſubject (ſee note, page 19, Vol. II.) before I had any knowledge of the practice of this Diſtrict. What I have ſince ſeen of it inclines me to decide in its favor. It is certainly more convenient to the farmer: and it is leſs degrading to the ſervants, than the practice of expoſing themſelves, for hire, in a public market; though it may not, perhaps, be ſo ſpeedy and certain a way of getting into place.

The WAGES OF SERVANTS, as thoſe of laborers, are low, compared with thoſe of moſt other Diſtricts. The yearly wages of men run

run from ſix to eight pounds; of women three pounds or three guineas.

The MODE OF TREATMENT OF FARM SERVANTS, here, may be ſaid to be a judicious mean between the extravagance of the Southern counties, and the oppoſite extreme of the Northern provinces.

III. APPRENTICES. It is a univerſal and common practice, throughout Devonſhire, and, I believe, the Weſt of England in general, to put out the children of paupers, boys more particularly, at the age of ſeven or eight years, to farmers and others; and to bind them, as apprentices, until they be twentyone years of age; and formerly until they were twentyfour! on condition of the maſter's finding them with every neceſſary, during the term of the apprenticeſhip.

This is an eaſy and ready way of diſpoſing of the children of paupers, and is fortunate for the children thus diſpoſed of; as enuring them to labor and induſtry, and providing them with better ſuſtenance, than

than they could expect to receive from their parents. To the farmers, too, such children, under proper tuition, might, one would think, be made highly valuable in their concerns, and, in the end, would become very profitable.

The contrary, however, is generally the case: an unfortunate and indeed lamentable circumstance, which arises, in a great measure, I apprehend, from improper treatment. Instead of treating them as their adopted children, or as relations, or as a superior order of servants, whose love and esteem they are desirous of gaining, for their mutual happiness, during the long term of their intimate connexion, as well as to secure their services at a time when they become the most valuable, they are treated, at least in the early stage of servitude, as the inferiors of yearly or weekly servants, are frequently subjected, I fear, to a state of the most abject drudgery: a severity which they do not forget, even should it be relaxed, as they grow up. the ordinary consequence is, no sooner are they capable of supporting themselves, than

than they desert their servitude, and fill the provincial Papers with advertisements for "runaway prentices."

There are, no doubt, circumstances under which it were difficult, or impossible, to render this class of servants, either pleasurable or profitable to their masters; such as the naturally bad disposition of the servants themselves, and the more reprehensible conduct of their parents, in giving them bad counsel. Nevertheless, it strikes me forcibly, that much might be done by a change of *principle*, in their treatment.

When the unfortunate offspring of unfortunate parents fall into the hands of men of sense and discretion, they frequently turn out well, and become most valuable members of the community.

A more *natural* seminary of working husbandmen could not be devised; and the progress in life, that some individuals of this class have made, is a recommendation of the practice; which, under the proper treatment of farmers, the encouragement of landlords, and the protection of Magistrates, might be profitably extended to other

other Diſtricts; and become a prolific ſource of the moſt valuable order of inhabitants a cultivated country can poſſeſs.

4.

BEASTS OF LABOR.

Introductory Remarks.

THE Diſtrict under ſurvey may be ſaid to be undergoing a change, with reſpect to this department of its Rural Economy: a change which has been going on, ſlowly, for the laſt twenty years; but which has, as yet, made little progreſs.

Formerly, CARRIAGE of every kind was done entirely on the BACKS OF HORSES; except in harveſt, when ſledges, drawn by oxen, were ſometimes uſed; alſo heaps of manure, in the field, were dragged abroad in ſmall cart ſledges, either by oxen or horſes. Twenty years ago, there was not a "pair of wheels" in the country; at leaſt not upon a farm; and nearly the ſame may be ſaid at preſent. Hay, corn, ſtraw, fuel, ſtones, dung, lime, &c. are, in the ordinary practice of the Diſtrict, ſtill carried on horſeback.

This, to a ſtranger, forms a ſtriking feature of management. Before the invention of wheel carriages, theſe modes of transfer were of courſe univerſal throughout the Iſland, and the reaſon of its being continued ſo long, in this Diſtrict, has no doubt been, in part, the unlevelneſs of its ſurface. But there are other Diſtricts, the cultured parts of whoſe ſurfaces are much ſteeper than thoſe of Devonſhire (for reaſons already given); and the continuance of the practice, here, has been in a great meaſure owing to a want of judgment in laying out roads; or a want of ſpirit in executing them; ariſing from a backwardneſs, in all matters of improvement. There are farms of ſome hundred acres, lying perfectly well for wheel carriages; as level as farms in general throughout the Iſland; yet have not a wheel carriage belonging to them.

I. It

I. It would be unfair, however, not to obſerve, that there are many farms in the Diſtrict, on which the uſe of "PACK HORSES" ought never to be laid wholly aſide. And, in many other Diſtricts, the ſame mode of conveyance might be partially adopted; for the diſpatch made, by pack horſes properly uſed, is ſuch as no one, who has not ſeen it, would readily apprehend * Nevertheleſs, the practice, compared with that of wheel carriages, in ſituations which will admit of them, is altogether ineligible; and the prevalence of it at preſent is a ſtrong proof of the

 back-

* In an inſtance noticed, in which a ſtout lad with two pack horſes, and two men with three horſes in a waggon, were carrying faggots nearly the ſame diſtance (the road of the one ſomewhat ſteep, of the other more level), the comparative diſpatch ſtood thus: Each pack horſe carried nine faggots (twelve are a full ſeam), and made eight journies a day; thus transferring twelve dozen. The waggon carried eight dozen at a load, and made ſix journies; and conſequently transferred juſt four times the number. But if the graſs horſes and the boy are calculated at ſixpence each, and the ſtable horſes and the men, at a ſhilling each, the diſparity of expence will not be found very conſiderable.

backward ſtate in which huſbandry ſtill remains, in this remote part of the Iſland.

II. OXEN have ever been the PLOW TEAM of the Diſtrict: ſometimes with horſes before them; but more generally alone: four aged oxen, or ſix growing ſteers, are the uſual "plow" of the Diſtrict.

Oxen are univerſally worked in YOKE; yet are remarkably tractable; and ſtep out with a pace, which a Kentiſh clown would think a hardſhip to follow, with his high-fed horſe team.

The ſtyle of DRIVING an Ox team, here, is obſervable; indeed, cannot paſs unnoticed by a ſtranger. The language, though in a great degree peculiar to the country, does not arreſt the attention; but the tone, or rather tune, in which it is delivered. It reſembles, with great exactneſs, the chantings, or recitative of the Cathedral ſervice. The plow boy chants the counter tenor, with unabated ardour through the day; the plowman throwing in, at intervals, his hoarſer notes. It is under-

underſtood that this chanting march, which may ſometimes be heard to a conſiderable diſtance, encourages and animates the team, as the muſic of a marching army, or the ſong of the rowers. Let this be as it may, I have never ſeen ſo much cheerfulneſs attending the operation of plowing, anywhere, as in Devonſhire.

The native BREED of this Diſtrict are ſomewhat too ſmall, for heavy work. But, in the North of the county, they are larger, and fitter for the yoke; and are, indeed, on the whole, the beſt working cattle I have anywhere ſeen. Theſe breeds will be ſpoken of, more fully, under the head CATTLE.

Oxen are here worked to a full AGE: ſometimes to ten or twelve years old.

I met with no SPAYED HEIFERS in the Diſtrict. The art of ſpaying does not appear to be known in the country.

III. CART HORSES, ſince the introduction of wheel carriages, are beginning to creep into the Diſtrict. They are moſtly of the black, heavy-heeled, unprofitable

fitable breed. However, in the ſteep pulls of this country, a true-drawn, ſteady kind is required; but the hardy active breed of Suffolk appears, to me, to be better calculated for the ſoil and ſurface of this country, than the ſluggiſh fen ſort, which is inſinuating itſelf into it.

But, in a country where draught oxen are of ſo excellent a quality, and where the drivers of ox teams are ſo expert, and at preſent ſo partial to them, it were pity almoſt to introduce any other animal of draught; unleſs under particular circumſtances *. It would be as direct an affront to a ſteady good ſervant, in this Diſtrict, to "ordain" him to go with a team of horſes, as

* I have ſeen a pair of young ſteers, riſing three years old, put before, as leaders, the ſecond or third day after they had been broken into yoke; and, in a few days more, made perfectly tractable, in this intellectual capacity.

The *goad* is the inſtrument uſed in driving, when oxen are uſed alone. But if horſes are uſed before them, a ſtrong kind of whip—a thong tied to the end of a pliant goad is the ordinary inſtrument—the identical "*gad*" which is uſed in Yorkſhire, when oxen and horſes are worked together, in a ſimilar manner.

as it would be to a Kentiſh plowman, to order him to take the charge of a team of oxen; and it might be a crime to do away ſo valuable a prejudice

The HOURS OF WORK are well regulated. The plowteams make two journies a day, as in Norfolk: they go out before eight in the morning, and return at twelve. Go out, again, before two, and return before ſix: working about eight hours a day.

5.

IMPLEMENTS.

IN a Diſtrict whoſe Rural Management is far behind that of many other parts of the Iſland, and whoſe preſent ſyſtem of practice is probably of very antient origin, we muſt expect to find a peculiarity, rather than an excellency, in its Implements of Huſbandry.

I. The WAGGONS which have been introduced, are of the Weſt-country con-

 ſtruction;

ſtruction; with the outer rail bending over the hind wheel; in the ſame manner as that of the Cotſwold waggon *: a peculiarity of conſtruction, which, I find, reaches from Glóceſterſhire to the landsend; and which, in much probability, has been originally copied from a two-wheel carriage, that is ſtill in uſe in Cornwall, and which may, poſſibly, have been heretofore common to the more Weſtern counties.

II. The CORNISH WAIN is among the ſimpleſt of wheel carriages. It is adapted either to oxen or horſes. It is a cart without a *body*; at leaſt without *ſides*; ſaving only two ſtrong bows, which bend over the wheels, to prevent the load from preſſing upon them. This Implement will be mentioned again in the MINUTES.

III. The DRAY, or SLEDGE, of this Diſtrict, is likewiſe found in the loweſt rank of ſimplicity. Merely two ſide pieces, joined

* See GLO. ECON. Vol. I. Page 57.

joined together with croſs bars. It is large, ſtrong, and uſeful, on many occaſions.

IV. The "GURRY-BUTT," or DUNG SLEDGE, of Devonſhire, is a ſort of ſliding cart, or barrow; uſually of a ſize proper to be drawn by one horſe: ſometimes it is made larger; I have ſeen four oxen drawing compoſt upon a fallow, in one of theſe little Implements; which might, anywhere, be made uſeful, on many occaſions; eſpecially in moving earth, ſtones, rubbiſh, or manure, a ſmall diſtance. The ſides and ends are about eighteen inches high, and are fixed; the load being diſcharged by overturning the carriage.

V. The FURNITURE OF PACK HORSES varies with the load to be carried. Hay, corn, ſtraw, faggots, and other comparatively light articles of burden, are loaded between "CROOKS;" formed of Willow poles, about the thickneſs of ſithe handles; and ſeven or eight feet long; bent as Ox bows; but with one end much longer than the other. Theſe are joined in in pairs, with ſlight croſs bars, eighteen inches to two feet long; and each horſe is furniſhed with two pair of theſe crooks; ſlung together, ſo as that the ſhorter and ſtronger ends ſhall lie eaſy and firmly againſt the pack ſaddle; the longer and lighter ends riſing, perhaps, fifteen or more inches, above the horſe's back, and ſtanding four or five feet from each other. Within, and between, theſe crooks, the load is piled, and bound faſt together, with that ſimplicity and diſpatch, which long practice ſeldom fails of ſtriking out.

Cordwood, large ſtones, and other heavy articles are carried between "SHORT CROOKS;" made of four natural bends or knees; both ends being nearly of the ſame length; and, in uſe, the points ſtand nearly level with the ridge of the pack ſaddle.

Dung, ſand, materials of buildings, roads, &c. &c. are carried in "POTTS;" or ſtrong coarſe panniers; ſlung together, like the crooks; and as panniers are uſually ſlung; the dung, eſpecially if long and light, being ridged up, over the ſaddle

The

The bottom of each pot is a falling door, on a ſtrong and ſimple conſtruction. The place of delivery being reached, the trap is unlatched, and the load releaſed.

Lime is univerſally carried in narrow BAGS; two or three of them being thrown acroſs a

PACKSADDLE; which is of wood, and of the ordinary conſtruction.

VI. The PLOW,--provincially "SEWL," pronounced "ZEWL,"—reſembles, in general appearance, the old-faſhioned Plows of other Diſtricts; but has three notable peculiarities of conſtruction. It has no rice or wreſt; the mold board ſtanding ſome inches above the level of the chip, head, ſoal, or keel of the Plow. This, in turning whole ground, is ſometimes an advantage; but, in a looſe fallow, ſuch a tool rather makes a rut than a furrow; half the ſoil, perhaps, remaining unſtirred.

Another variation in the conſtruction of the Devonſhire Plow is ſtill more ſingular. The ſheath, breaſt, or ſtem is not fixed in the beam; but ſerves as a regulator to the depth

depth of the furrow; and is made longer or ſhorter, at the will of the Plowman; who faſtens it, in the required poſition, with a wedge, driven into a notch, made acroſs the end of the tenon, above the beam.

The third peculiarity of conſtruction lies in uniting the principal handle to the ſoal, chip, or keel. In moſt old Plows, this handle is tenoned into the ſoal. But, here, the foot of the handle is crooked; ſhooting horizontally forward, in a line parallel with the ſoal; to which it is ſtrongly faſtened, by two thick wooden pins driven through them.

In caſes, where the old faſhioned ſoal is uſed, this is an admirable way of joining the handle -to it; giving great ſtrength and firmneſs of conſtruction. There is ſome difficulty in finding pieces of wood, fit for this ſort of handle; but, in converting top wood, the eye of a good Plowwright is ever on the watch for them. For further remarks on this Implement, ſee the Minutes.

VII. The

VII. The rough HARROWS of this Country---provincially "Drags" --- consist of two parts; each of three beams; hung together with hooks and eyes; and drawn by the corner of the foremost. They hang remarkably steady behind the team.

VIII. The ROLLER of this District has not yet been furnished with shafts, or a pole, to check it in going down-hill; notwithstanding the unlevelness of surface!

IX. The "DRUDGE" is an Implement peculiar, I believe, to this part of the Island. It is a long, heavy, wooden-toothed rake; with the teeth broad, and set with the flat side foremost; drawn by oxen or horses, and used to collect the fragments of sward, loosened by the plow and harrow; for the purpose of burning it, in the manner which will be hereafter described, under the article SODBURNING.

X. The YOKE of Devonshire is of too valuable a construction to be passed without

out notice. It is by far the beſt I have anywhere ſeen. It is at once light, and eaſy, to the animal. The operative part of the WOODWORK, that which reſts upon the withers of the Ox, is broad and gently convex on the under ſide, to ſit eaſy; and hollowed out, above, to give it lightneſs. To prevent this thin part from being ſplit by the action of the bows in work, rivets are or ought to be run through it, horizontally, cloſe to the outer ſides of the bow holes. The ſpecies of wood is chiefly *Alder*, ſometimes *Elm*.

Another moſt admirable part, in the conſtruction of this Yoke, belongs to the DRAUGHT IRON; which, inſtead of having, as is uſual, a ſingle ſtaple or eye, to receive the ring; the crown of the ſtaple is enlarged, and is divided into three compartments or notches, like thoſe of the draught iron of a plow; in order to give the weaker Ox the requiſite advantage. An admirable thought; and equally good in theory and in practice.

The BOWS are invariably, I believe, of *Elm*; being brought from the Exeter quarter

quarter of the County, into this Diſtrict: ſelling, here, at about 18d. a pair: while the neighbourhood abounds in *Aſh* and *Sallow*, with which the farmers might make their own bows, or have them made, at much leſs expence.

XI. Some of the TOOLS of this Country are not leſs peculiar, than are many of its Implements. The SHOVEL is pointed, in the manner of the hay ſpade of the North of England; reſembling the marks on the ſuit of ſpades, in playing cards: a circumſtantial evidence, this, that the tool under notice was once the common ſpade or ſhovel of the Iſland at large * In this part of it, it ſtill ſupplies the place of both ſpade and ſhovel: there being no ſuch tool as either a ſpade or a ſhovel, of the ordinary conſtruction, in the hands of farmers or their laborers. I have traced this tool as far eaſtward as Wiltſhire. In Dorſetſhire, it is common.

It is furniſhed with a long, ſtrong, crooked

* Or are both Cards and pointed Shovels of *French* origin?

crooked handle, the back of the bend being turned upward; and, in uſing it, the hollow of the bend is reſted upon the thigh, which is uſually guarded with a ſhield of ſtrong leather, bound upon it.

This tool has many good properties. It enters any ſubſtance much eaſier than a broad-mouthed ſhovel or ſpade; and anſwers, in the hands of a Weſtcountry man, every purpoſe of the ſhovel, the ſpade, the yard ſcraper, and the dung fork of other Diſtricts. As a ſubſtitute for the laſt, however, it is leſs eligible, than it is for the three firſt.

There are various other peculiarities, in the ſhape and dimenſions of Tools; but none of them are ſufficiently excellent, or ſtriking, to be noticed here. Some of them may, nevertheleſs, be mentioned, in treating of the operations to which they belong. Thoſe which are here brought forward are ſufficient to ſhew, demonſtrably, that the Rural Management of this quarter of the Iſland has either had a ſeparate origin, or has not partaken of the improvements and changes which that of the reſt

reſt of the kingdom has undergone. Implements and utenſils of huſbandry, as of war, are among the beſt evidences of Hiſtory.

6.

THE WEATHER.

THE CLIMATURE, or general ſtate of the weather, in this extreme part of the Iſland, has been already ſpoken of. And with reſpect to PROGNOSTICS, or a foreknowledge of the weather, at any time or ſeaſon, I have gained no information, here. The BAROMETER appears to be little attended to; and, indeed, all thoughts about the weather, even of the morrow or the paſſing day, are conſidered as uſeleſs; until the miſty ſummit of ſome oraeular mountain announces approaching rain.

It may be true, that, in this peninſular ſituation, the weather is leſs certain, than in the more central parts of the Iſland; yet, from the obſervations I had an opportunity of making, I found the BAROMETER,

 and

and the SETTING SUN to be of the ſame or a ſimilar uſe, here, in forming a judgement of the weather, as I have ever found them, in other places; though, in this country, which may be ſaid to be ſituated within the region of rain, the changes from fair to foul weather are, no doubt, more ſudden, than they are, in more eaſterly and central ſituations. Nevertheleſs, I am clearly of opinion, that a due attention to the barometer and the ſetting ſun, in the ſummer months, would amply repay the occupiers of lands, for the time and attention they might have occaſion to beſtow upon them.

7.

PLAN OF THE MANAGEMENT OF FARMS.

PREFATORY REMARKS.

AN account of the RISE AND PROGRESS of AGRICULTURE, in the ſeveral Diſtricts of of the Iſland, would form an intereſting part of its HISTORY.

That the Rural Managements, now found in different Provinces, have had diſtinct origins, or have been raiſed to the ſtates in which we now ſeverally find them, by very different circumſtances, is moſt evident. But whether the obvious diſtinctions, which now appear, have ariſen, from the circumſtance of the firſt ſettlers of the Iſland having migrated from different countries; or from that of ſubſequent conquerors having introduced their reſpective ſyſtems; or that of improvements having taken different routes, in different Diſtricts, —is by no means a queſtion that can be promptly anſwered.

By comparing minute details of the practices of different Provinces, with the minutiæ of practice, obſervable in the ſeveral Countries of the Continent, ſomething might be determined reſpecting this ſubject.

That the outlines of Management, in different parts, have ariſen, in ſome meaſure, out of the nature of ſoils, and the ſtate of occupancy in which they have happened to be placed, is probable, from the ſtriking fact, that the general Plan of Management, now practiſed in the Diſtrict under view, is, in outline, the ſame as that of the Midland Diſtrict, ſituated at two hundred miles diſtance, and ſevered from it by Diſtricts purſuing contrary practices. Both of them have been ſome length of time in a ſtate of incloſure; both of them are productive either of corn or graſs; and both of them have fallen into that routine of Management, which, viewed in the outline, will not, perhaps, admit of much improvement: namely, that of ſubjecting the lands in general to an alternacy of corn and graſs; but preſerving the bottoms of vallies and dips, in a ſtate of perennial graſs or meadow land. And, what is remarkable, theſe lands, in both Diſtricts, have been watered, time out of mind: but with this ſtill more remarkable difference, the one was wholly overflowed, and kept covered with ſtagnant water, the other irrigated

gated with running water,---agreeably to the practice of the South of Europe.

From this and other circumſtances, which will appear in the courſe of this Survey, it is *probable*, that the Rural Management of the Weſt of England is of *French* origin.

To aſſiſt us in gaining a general idea of the Plan of Management of this Diſtrict it will be proper to view

I. The preſent Objects of its Huſbandry.

II. The Courſe of Practice, whereby theſe Objects are attained.

I. The preſent OBJECTS of Huſbandry in Weſt Devonſhire; thoſe from which the Farmer expects to draw rent, labor, and perſonal income;—are

Corn, and, of late years,
Potatoes,
Fruit Liquor,
Dairy Produce,
Cows,
Oxen,
Sheep,
Swine.

The CROPS, at preſent in cultivation, are principally,

Wheat, and
Barley; with ſome
Oats; a very few
Peas; ſome
Turneps; many
Potatoes; with at preſent much
Cloverand RayGraſs; together with
Meadow Graſs,
Paſture Land Produce, and
Fruit.

The LIVESTOCK of the Diſtrict are

Working Horſes;--- a few
Rearing Horſes,
Working Oxen,
Dairy Cows,
Rearing Cattle,
Grazing Cattle,
Swine,
Breeding Ewes,
Store Sheep,
Fatting Sheep,
Rabbits,
Poultry.

II. COURSE

II. COURSE OF PRACTICE. Left it ſhould be ſaid that the Practice of a Country, ſo far behind the reſt of the Kingdom, in Rural Improvements, as that which is now under view, cannot be a fit ſubject of minute deſcription, it may here be proper to remark, that the Subject of Agriculture, viewed to its outmoſt limits, is not only extenſive, but abſtruſe; and that no ESTABLISHED PRACTICE can be ſo inconſiderable as not to furniſh uſeful ideas, if fairly diſcuſſed. Beſide, we have ſeen that the outline of its Plan of Management is in ſome meaſure right, and, by due inveſtigation, we may be able to detect minutial practices, which will throw freſh light on the general ſubject.

It has been mentioned, as the Practice of this Diſtrict, to keep the cultured lands, alternately, in ley graſſes and arable crops. The latter have long been fixed and invariable; but the number of years allowed for the duration of the former depends on circumſtances, and the judgement of individuals. Speaking generally of the Diſtrict, more than half of its cultured lands are in temporary ley: besides the perennial leys or meadow lands; and beside the rough pasture grounds that are not under regular cultivation.

Dividing the arable lands into ten parts, five of these parts may, in giving a general idea of their arrangement, be said to be in ley or pasture grounds, one under preparation for wheat, one in wheat, one in barley, one in oats, and one in ray grass and clover; following each other in the SUCCESSION, in which they are here set down: namely,

Pasture,
Partial Fallow, or Beat-burning,
Wheat,
Barley,
Oats,
Herbage.

This has been the ordinary Course of Management, during the last fifty or sixty years; during which length of time, I understand, herbage has been, more or less, *cultivated:* a circumstance which does credit to the Rural Management of the Country.

About

About twenty years ago, the cultivation of the POTATOE was introduced into this Diſtrict; and TURNEPS have been more or leſs cultivated, for a much longer time; but not in a manner which redounds any honor on their cultivators.

Theſe two crops, being grown on ley grounds, have broken in upon the prior ſyſtem of Management: ſo that, at this juncture, the Diſtrict may be ſaid to be without any regular Courſe of Management; and it muſt remain in this predicament, until turneps and potatoes ſhall be introduced after wheat or oats, as a fallow crop for barley and ley herbage.

8.

MANAGEMENT OF THE SOIL.

IN this department of the arable Management, the Huſbandry of Weſt Devonſhire

ſhire is very defective. The lands, in general, are foul and OUT OF TILTH. The leys are many of them covered with fern and thiſtles, a few years after they are laid down to graſs, as if they had been, for ages, in a ſtate of commonage; and, when broken up, are equally diſgraced by myriads of ſeed weeds.

This foul ſtate of the Soil is not more owing to the ſmall number of PLOWINGS it receives, than to the defect, which has been mentioned, in the conſtruction of the PLOW, and the injudicious manner of uſing it. The plit, or plowſlice, is carried too wide; the ſhare is narrow, and the ſtern of the plow without a wreſt to force open the furrow. Hence, in plowing broken ground, half the weeds are left uncut, and the lower part of the ſoil left almoſt wholly unſtirred; the moldboard only ſliding off the upper part; thus covering up the uncut weeds, and giving the land the *appearance* of having been plowed. The conſequence is, the weeds ſoon break through their thin covering, and take again full poſſeſſion of the ſurface. I have ſeen turneps, after a fallow

fallow of three or four plowings, overshaded with fern a foot high, before the turnep plants were fit for the hoe.

Another cause of imperfect tillage, in this District, is the UNRECLAIMED state in which much of its arable lands remain, with respect to large stones, and rocky obstructions of the plow; and which want nothing but spirit and industry to remove them; so as to give an even and sufficient depth of furrow.

The Devonshire Plowmen, however, have hit upon a much easier way of saving their plows from destruction and themselves from injury, than that of clearing the soil from stones. Instead of using an iron bolt, to fasten the draught chain to the end of the beam, a wooden pin is substituted. When the share strikes against a stone, the pin breaks; and by this simple contrivance the neck of the plow and the teeth of the Plowman are freed from danger.

It is probable that, formerly, much has been done towards CLEARING THE GROUND FROM OBSTRUCTIONS OF THE PLOW; as a very ingenious method of freeing

freeing the ſoil from large hard detached ſtones has been introduced into practice: namely, that of *ſinking* them below the ſoil; ſo as to give free range for the plow, above them. This is done by digging pits beneath them: an operation, however, which is ſomewhat dangerous, and requires a degree of care and circumſpection.

CLEANSING SOIL FROM SEED WEEDS. I muſt not omit to mention, here, an incident of practice, which was related to me, in this Diſtrict, by a friend of the farmer in whoſe practice it occurred. A field, particularly *ſubject to wild oats*, was effectually freed from them, by dunging it well, while under fallow, and by working it afterwards, ſo as to mix the ſoil and dung intimately together. The conſequence of this was a full crop of oats; which was mown for hay; and the ſoil ever after freed from theſe troubleſome weeds.

This incident, though not, perhaps, accurately ſtated (it is not probable that, with the imperfect tillage of this country, every individual ſeed ſhould be brought at once into vegetation) ſhews the utility of

WORKING

WORKING A DUNGED FALLOW, before the crop be ſown: a practice I have ever found highly eligible.

SODBURNING. The moſt noticeable particular of Management, in the Soil Proceſs of this Diſtrict, is that of "BURNING BEAT," as it is provincially termed; anſwering to the paring and burning, or more technically, ſodburning—of other Diſtricts.

This operation in Agriculture has been practiſed, in this Weſtern part of the Iſland, from time beyond which memory nor tradition reaches. It has probably been imported from the oppoſite ſhore of the Continent.

In an old tract which I ſaw, ſome years ago, in the Britiſh Muſeum, this operation is termed DEVONSHIRING, and it is to this day called Denſhiring, in different Diſtricts.

There are, at preſent, three diſtinct methods of ſeparating the ſward or ſod, provincially the "ſpine"—from the ſoil. The one is performed with a "BEATING AXE"—namely a large adze—ſome five or ſix inches wide, and ten or twelve inches long; crooked, and ſomewhat hollow or diſhing. With this, which was probably the original inſtrument employed in the operation, large chips, ſhavings, or ſods are ſtruck off. It is ſtill uſed in rough uneven grounds, eſpecially where furze or the ſtubs of bruſhwood abound. In uſing it, the workman appears, to the eye of a ſtranger at ſome diſtance, to be *beating* the ſurface, as with a beetle, rather than to be chipping off the ſward with an edge-tool. This operation is termed "HAND BEATING."

The next Inſtrument in uſe is the "SPADE," reſembling the paring ſpade, or breaſt plow, of other Diſtricts: with, however, in ſome inſtances at leaſt, a notable addition: namely a moldboard! fixed in ſuch a manner, as to turn the ſod or turf, as a plow turns the furrow ſlice: thus becoming literally a BREAST PLOW; a name which has probably been given to the Implement in this ſtate; and continued to be applied to the ſpade or ſhare, after the moldboard was laid aſide.

In

In working with this tool, the laborer proceeds without ſtopping to divide the ſods into ſhort lengths; this part being done by women and children; who follow, to break the turf into lengths, and ſet the pieces on edge to dry.

The PRICE for "SPADING" is about three halfpence, a ſquare perch, of 18 feet, or ſixteen or ſeventeen ſhillings a ſtatute acre.

Formerly, it is probable, this inſtrument was much in uſe; but, at preſent, it appears to be chiefly in the hands of ſmall farmers.

The inſtrument at preſent uſed, for ſeparating the ſpine or graſſy turf from the ſoil, by farmers in general, is the common TEAM PLOW, with ſome little alteration in the ſize and form of the ſhare; according to the fancy or judgement of the farmer or his plowman; there being two different ways of performing the operation. The one is termed "Velling," the other "Skirting," or "Skirwinking"

For VELLING, the ſhare is made wide, with the angle or outer point of the wing or fin turned upward, to ſeparate the turf entirely from the ſoil.

For

For SKIRTING, the common ſhare is uſed; but made, perhaps, ſomewhat wider than when it is uſed in the ordinary operation of plowing.

In this mode of uſing the plow, little more than half the ſward is pared off; turning the part raiſed; upon a line of unmoved turf; as in the operation of ribbing, rice-balking, raftering, or half plowing. The paring of turf in this caſe is from one to two inches thick, on the coulter margin, decreaſing in thickneſs to a thin feather edge, by which it adheres to the unmoved ſward.

Having lain ſome time in this ſtate, to rot or grow tender, it is pulled to pieces with rough *harrows*, drawn acroſs the lines of turf; and, having lain in this rough ſtate, until it be ſufficiently dry, it is bruiſed with a *roller*, and immediately harrowed, with lighter harrows; walking the horſes one way, and trotting them the other; to ſhake the earth out more effectually from among the roots of the graſs; going over the ground again, and perhaps again, according to the ſeaſon, and the judgement of the

the manager; until moſt of the earth be diſengaged.

The "BEAT," or fragments of turf, being ſufficiently dry, it is gathered into heaps of five or ſix buſhels each; either with the "DRUDGE," mentioned under the Section Implements, firſt into rows, and then, drawing it along the rows, into heaps; or is pulled together with long-toothed HAND RAKES, adapted to the purpoſe. The former is more expeditious, and requires fewer hands; the latter gathers the beat cleaner,—freer from earth; which is liable to be drawn together by the drudge.

The "BEAT BURROWS," or heaps, being rounded, and ſhook up light and hollow, a wiſp of rough ſtraw,—a large handful,—is thruſt, double, into the windward ſide of each heap: and, a number of heaps being thus primed, a match or flambeau is formed, with "reed" or ſtraight unthraſhed ſtraw; one end of which being lighted, it is applied, in ſucceſſion, to the looſe ragged ends of the wiſps of ſtraw; which readily communicate the fire to the heaps.

The center of the heaps being consumed, the outskirts are thrown lightly into the dimples or hollows, and the heaps rounded up, as at first; continuing to right up the burrows until the whole of the beat be consumed, or *changed*, by the action of the fire.

The produce of the first skirting being burnt, and spread over the surface, the operation is sometimes repeated; by running the plow across the lines of the first skirting: thus paring off the principal part of the spine; again dragging, rolling, harrowing, collecting, and burning, as in the former operation.

General Remarks on Sodburning.

HAVING formerly spoken, at some length, on the subject now under notice, the less is requisite to be said in this place*. Nevertheless, the practice of this country (to which I was a stranger when I wrote the remarks above referred to), tending to confirm the ideas which are there offered; and

* See York Econ. Vol. I. page 311.

and this Diſtrict being, in all probability, the fountain and ſource of the practice, in theſe kingdoms, it would be improper to diſmiſs a topic, which is of conſiderable importance to the rural concerns of the Iſland, without taking a retroſpective view of the practice, in this quarter of it.

There needs not a better proof, that the practice, under the guidance of diſcretion, is not *deſtructive* to ſoils, nor any way *dangerous* to Agriculture; than the fact, ſo fully aſcertained here, that after a conſtant uſe of it, during, perhaps, a long ſucceſſion of ages, the ſoil ſtill continues to be productive; and, under management in other reſpects much below par, continues to yield a rent equivalent to that drawn from lands of equal quality, in more enligntened Diſtricts: and there appears to me ſtrong reaſon to imagine, that, *under the preſent courſe of management*, ſodburning is eſſential to ſucceſs. Indeed, inſtances are mentioned, and pretty well authenticated, in which men who ſtood high in their profeſſion, and of ſufficient capitals, having been injured or brought to poverty, through their being reſtricted from this practice; which may be ſaid to form a principal wheel in the preſent machine or ſyſtem of the Devonſhire huſbandry. For it is obſervable, that the Wheat crops of this Diſtrict, after the burning, liming, and one plowing, which will be mentioned in deſcribing the culture of that crop, notwithſtanding the accumulated foulneſs of the ſoil, already deſcribed, are, in general, beautifully clean: and this, though the ſucceeding crop of Barley may be foul in the extreme: a circumſtance, perhaps, which would be difficult to account for, in any other way, than in the check which the weeds receive, from the burning. The imperfect tillage, of one plowing and a chopping, cannot be allowed to have any ſhare, in producing this huſbandlike effect.

Let it not, however, be underſtood, that any facts, which are here brought forward, are intended to ſhew the *neceſſity* of ſod-burning, in this or any other Diſtrict. To three fourths of the Iſland, the practice may be ſaid to be unknown; yet in many parts of this unburnt ſurface of country, if not through-

throughout the whole of it, the preſent ſtate of huſbandry is preferable to that of Devonſhire; and, whenever CLEAN FALLOWS, and ſuitable FALLOW CROPS, ſhall be introduced, here, and judiciouſly mixed with the grain crops, agreeably to the practice of modern huſbandry, burning beat will certainly be no longer required.

In fact, the upland ſoils of this country are not adapted to the practice. The ſoil under ordinarily good management, is, in its nature, productive of clean ſweet herbage; and, under a proper courſe of huſbandry, never would become coarſe and rough ſkinned, ſo as to require this operation; which is, as has heretofore been remarked, peculiarly adapted to old coarſe tough ſward, whether of dry land or wet, light land or ſtiff; and, in much probability, to cold retentive ſoils, as often as a ſuitable rotation of crops will permit *

That burning the graſſy ſward of land acts as a STIMULUS to the ſoil is everywhere obſervable: in this Diſtrict, I ſaw a

 ſtriking

* See YORK. ECON. Vol. I. Page 313.

ſtriking inſtance of it. A meagre thin-ſoiled ſwell, never worth half a crown an acre, has, by burning and liming, been ſtimulated to throw out, part after part, ample crops of wheat: which, however, were found to exhauſt the ſoil, ſo compleatly, that no after crops of grain were attempted; but the land was ſuffered to lay down again to reſt, and yet remains in a ſtate of ſtill leſs value, perhaps, than it was in, before it was broken up for wheat.

This, however, is not an evidence againſt the operation of ſodburning; but the reverſe. The value of the wheat, thus produced, was probably equal to that of the fee ſimple of the land it grew on; which, if a grateful return, of part of this value received, had been made, would probably have been put into a much better ſtate than it was in, before it underwent this profitable operation.

Does not lime, when uſed alone, act as a ſtimulus? Does not tillage act as a ſtimulus? Yet will any one aſſert that calcareous earths and tillage are unfriendly to agriculture?

From

From what I have ſeen, in this country, of the effects of ſodburning, I am more and more convinced, that, in many caſes, and under diſcrete management, it forms a valuable part of Britiſh huſbandry; and may become an inſtrument of real improvement, in places where it is not, at preſent, known; eſpecially in bringing the WASTE LANDS of the Iſland into a proper courſe of cultivation *.

POLITICAL AGRICULTURE appears to me to be highly intereſted, in the continuance of this practice; which men, who farm in cloſets, ſeem deſirous to extinguiſh. But let them theorize with caution; and go forth into the field of practice, before they venture to draw inferences, which may prove ſubverſive of the public good they doubtleſs intend to promote.

Men of landed property, however, ought to regard this practice, with a watchful eye. Through its means, a tenant has it in his power to enrich him-

 ſelf,

* For remarks on the means of CULTIVATIN WASTE LANDS, ſee YORK. ECON. Vol. I. P. 316.

ſelf, at the expence of his landlord. And although, while he is doing this, he may be enriching the Public; yet proprietors, conſidered as ſuch, have an undoubted right to guard their property. But let them not, by an ill judged and narrow-minded policy, injure, at once, the Public, their tenants, and themſelves. It may be prudent to reſtrict tenants, in certain caſes, from the uſe of this practice; but to debar them from it, in all caſes, would be equally impolitic, as to reſtrict them from the uſe of calcareous earths; or, as is too often the caſe, to debar them from the uſe of the plow, where the application of it would be beneficial to themſelves, to their tenants, and to the community. This is, in truth, laying up their talents in napkins.

IN EVERY CASE, IN WHICH A LANDLORD GIVES UP SPECIAL ADVANTAGES TO A TENANT, HE OUGHT TO BE PAID DOWN A REASONABLE CONSIDERATION FOR SUCH ADVANTAGES; OR THE TENANT SHOULD BIND HIMSELF TO PAY, DURING A SUITABLE TERM, AN EQUIVALENT RENT.

9.

MANURES AND THEIR MANAGEMENT.

THE manures, at present in use, are
Dung,
Sea sand, and
Lime.

I. DUNG. This is either YARD DUNG, or PLYMOUTH DUNG; the latter arising from the scrapings of the streets, with dung and offal of every kind, which populous towns afford, and which, when applied to lands that have not been accustomed to additions of that nature, never fail of producing the most favorable effect.

In regard to the RAISING OF DUNG, in this District, I have met with nothing com-

commendable. Farm yards are without form, and unguarded from extraneous water: nor are they supplied with mold or other absorbent substances, to imbibe and retain the superfluous juices of the dung.

II. SEA SAND. This has been a manure of the District, beyond memory, or tradition.

There are two SPECIES still in use. The one bearing the ordinary appearances of sea sand, as found at the mouths of rivers; namely a compound of the common sand and mud. The other appears, to the eye, clean fragments of broken shells, without mixture; resembling, in colour and particles, clean-dressed bran of wheat.

By analysis, one hundred grains of the former contain about thirty grains of common siliceous sea sand, with a few grains of fine silt or mud; the rest is calcareous earth, mixed with the animal matter of marine shells.

One hundred grains of the latter contain eightyfive grains of the matter of shells,

ſhells, and fifteen grains of an earthy ſubſtance, which reſembles, in colour and particles, minute fragments of burnt clay, or common red brick.

Theſe ſands are raiſed in different parts of Plymouth Sound, or in the harbour; and are carried up the eſtuaries, in barges; and from theſe, on horſeback, perhaps five or ſix miles, into the country; of courſe at a very great expence: yet without diſcrimination, by men in general, as to their ſpecific qualities. The ſhelly kind, no doubt, brought them into repute, and induced landlords to bind their tenants to the uſe of them; but without ſpecifying the ſort; and the bargemen, of courſe, bring ſuch as they can raiſe, and convey, at the leaſt labor and expence *.

But the uſe of ſea ſand has been for ſome time

* It is probable that the ſpecimen firſt mentioned, is above par, as to quality. I have ſeen ſand of a much *cleaner* appearance, travelling towards the fields of this quarter of the country: and, near Biddeford, in North Devonſhire, I collected a ſpecimen, under the operation of "melling" with mold, which contains eighty grains percent of clean ſiliceous ſand!

time on the decline in this quarter of the county, and is now in a great meaſure ſuperſeded, by

III. LIME. This ſpecies of manure, I underſtand, has been more or leſs uſed, here, for about ſixty years: a proof that, heretofore, the Weſt of England ſtood forward in Rural Improvements.

The only SPECIES in uſe is burnt from a variegated STONE, or marble, raiſed near Plymouth; and carried up the different eſtuaries; along the banks, and at the heads of which there are kilns; in which great quantities are burnt, by men who make a buſineſs of burning it.

The LIME KILNS of Devonſhire are large, and of an expenſive conſtruction; ſome of them coſting not leſs than thirty or forty pounds each. But their duration is in proportion: one which has been built thirty years is ſtill firm and ſound on the outſide. The walls are of extraordinary thickneſs; wide enough, on the top, for horſes to paſs round the kiln, and deliver the ſtones.

The

The body or inſide of the Devonſhire kiln is not well formed. The ſides are too ſtraight: the cavity is not ſufficiently eggſhaped,—is too conical,—too narrow in the middle,—the contents, of courſe, hang,—do not ſettle down freely and evenly,—as they do in a well ſhaped kiln. The rim is guarded with a curb of large moorſtones.

The ſtones are brought up from the water ſide, on horſeback, or upon aſſes; and, being diſtributed round the top of the kiln, are there broken, and thrown into the kiln with ſhovels; without the extra trouble of carrying them in baſkets: a ſaving, probably, which counterbalances the apparently extra expence of carrying up the unbroken ſtones, on horſeback, inſtead of in carts: ſo that we have, here, as in many other inſtances, in Rural Management, two roads, of ſimilar length and expediency, leading to the ſame end.

The FUEL chiefly, or wholly, *Welſh culm*.

Lime is SEPARATED into two ſorts, at the kiln. Thoſe who carry it to a great diſ-

diſtance, on horſeback, take only the clean knobs, or "STONE LIME;" the aſhes and rubbiſh being ſold, at a lower price, to thoſe who have lands at a ſhorter diſtance from the kilns, under the name of "LIME ASHES" This is a very accurate practice, when lime is carried to a great diſtance.

Upon the whole, the manufacturing of lime may be ſaid to be well conducted, in this country; and the PREPARATION of it, for manure, is entitled, at leaſt on the ſcore of induſtry, to ſtill higher praiſe, and to a minute deſcription.

Previous to fetching the lime, "earth ridges" are formed in the field; either with mold hacked from the borders of it, or with the ſoil of the area, raiſed with the plow. The earth thus raiſed is broken into ſmall fragments, and formed into long narrow beds. Upon theſe earth ridges the ſtone lime is laid; and covered up with the outſkirts of the beds.

When the lime has burſt the covering, and is found to be ſufficiently fallen, the ridges

ridges are "melled;" the earth and lime are intimately mixed together; in a very ingenious and effectual manner. The workman begins at one end of the ridge; and, with a hack or ſingle-ended mattock, hacks down the heap; mixing the whole intimately, by beating it with the *ſide* of the hack; raiſing it up again with the point, and again hitting it ſideway, with a ſlight and dexterity to be acquired only by practice. When the two ingredients are ſufficiently blended, the compoſt is thrown back, with a ſhovel, and formed into a roof-like heap; ſtill continuing to burſt any lumps the hack had miſſed, with the back of the ſhovel, and to mingle the parts as evenly as poſſible.

In theſe ridges the compoſt remains, until the time of ſpreading.

Lime compoſt is SPREAD from the ridges, or angular heaps above deſcribed, by means of gurry buts, or of wheelbarrows. When the latter are uſed, it is proper to harrow and roll the ſurface, before the operation commences.

GENERAL

General Remarks on the Application of Lime as a Manure.

THE right application of lime to the soil, has long appeared to me a subject which deserves the strictest investigation. In Norfolk, marl being the prevailing calcareous manure, I paid the less attention to lime. In Yorkshire, lime has long been depended upon, as a principal agent, in the production of arable crops. In that District, therefore, I paid much attention to the subject *. In Glocestershire, it can scarcely be said to enter into the list of manures. But, in the Midland Counties, it has, for some time past, been in full estimation; and some considerable attention is paid to its application; especially in watering and turning over the load heaps, before they are spread out upon the soil †.

In the application of lime to soil, as a manure, the perfection of management appears

* See York. Econ. Vol. I. P. 349.

† See Mid. Econ. Vol. I. P. 201.

appears to be, from what is at preſent publicly known on the ſubject, the incorporation of the two ſubſtances, into one homogeneous maſs; or, at leaſt, to mix the Lime, in a ſtate of powder, with ſome portion of ſoil, in order to ſeparate its particles, and prevent their adhering in lumps, and returning, in this form, to a ſtate of chalk or marl: for although Lime reduced to that ſtate may not be loſt to the ſoil, as a manure, it probably does not act as *Lime*, but as *Marl*; and, of courſe, a given quantity of Lime, laid on in whole ſtones or large fragments, will not produce the ſame effect, in a given time, as it would have done, had it been more evenly diſtributed,---more mechanically aſſimilated with the ſoil.

There are two widely differing methods of effecting this mechanical union. The one is to reduce the ſoil to a fine tilth; to ſpread the Lime evenly over it, in a ſtate of powder; and to mix them together, WITH THE ROLLER AND HARROW, until the whiteneſs of the Lime diſappears: ſuffering them to remain in this ſtate, if the ſeaſon will admit of it, until a fall of rain has ſtill more intimately united the two ſubſtances.

The other method is to mix the Lime, BY HAND, with a certain portion of ſoil collected for that purpoſe; agreeably to the practice of the Diſtrict under review.

In a favorable climate; in the ſummer ſeaſon: and where a ſufficient quantity of Lime can be readily collected; there can be no doubt as to the ſuperiority of the firſt method: it is more expeditious, much leſs expenſive, and infinitely more compleat.

But, in a leſs certain climate and ſeaſon; and where the buſineſs of fetching Lime goes on ſlowly, — continuing, perhaps, through the ſummer months, the Devonſhire practice, unleſs the Lime were lodged under cover, until the land were ready to receive it, is certainly the moſt eligible. The great objection to it is the labor and expence which it incurs. The "hacking of vorrage" --- the forming of "earth ridges," the "melling," and "ſetting about lime and earth" may be ſaid to employ

employ a ſet of laborers the ſummer through.

Experiencing the tediouſneſs and inconveniency of theſe operations, and ſeeing the wetneſs and uncertainty of the climate, with reſpect to "burning Beat," it ſtruck me that much time would be ſaved, and a degree of certainty gained, by uniting the two operations of preparing Lime and burning Beat: namely, by burning the Beat with the Lime; and by mixing the Lime with the aſhes and ſoil of the Beat: thus ſaving, on either hand, much labor; ſetting the ſeaſon, as it were, at defiance (for the wetter the Beat the quicker would be the operation of the Lime); and, at the ſame time, deſtroying the roots and ſeeds of weeds, with the eggs of inſects and animalcula of various kinds, and this *perhaps* with leſs injury to the vegetable matter of the Beat, than by the ordinary proceſs of combuſtion. Strongly impreſſed with theſe ideas, I ſet about carrying them into execution. The reſult will appear, in the MINUTES.

10.

SEMINATION.

I GATHERED no general information, reſpecting this department of the arable Management, in the Diſtrict under view. Every thing is ſown broadcaſt. A modern drill made its appearance ſome years ago; but it has been laid aſide.

The method of ſeminating the Wheat crop, here, is ſingular. It will appear in its place; under the head WHEAT.

11.

THE MANAGEMENT OF GROWING CROPS.

THE Management of Crops during their Growth, is confined to HAND-WEEDING, which is performed with ordinary

dinary care. The HOING of Field Crops has not yet been introduced: not even for TURNEPS! as will appear under that head.

The VERMIN of ARABLE CROPS are below par, in number and deſtructiveneſs.

GAME is kept within bounds: there are few Hares, and no Pheaſants.

PIGEONS are not numerous.

ROOKS, in ſome places, are evidently too numerous.

SPARROWS are in conſiderable number; and require to be checked: a buſineſs which reſts with Farmers; who can have no color of complaint againſt Gentlemen for encouraging Rooks, while the more injurious Sparrows are ſuffered to remain in force.

WILD DEER were formerly common, in the woods of this Diſtrict, and were found very injurious to the verging crops. But, through the good offices of the late Duke of Bedford, the country is now nearly free from them.

12.

HARVESTING.

THE Harveſt Management, at preſent eſtabliſhed in the Diſtrict, has evidently riſen out of the practice of carrying home harveſt produce on horſeback. For although this practice has in ſome degree been laid aſide, the operations of Harveſt (that of carrying excepted) are the ſame as they were, before the introduction of wheel carriages.

Every article of corn produce is BOUND, even the rakings of barley and oats that have been mown! But this, in the horſeback huſbandry, was perfectly right. Sheaves, or bundles of any ſort, are not only much fitter for loading between crooks, but are handier to be pitcht, or rather flung, from the ground or floor, to the top of the rick or mow, in the manner that will be deſcribed, than looſe corn.

I have

I have ſeen rakings waſted; becauſe there was not time to bind them, before the rain ſet in; though waggons were ſtanding by, to receive them.

Formerly, it ſeems, looſe corn, which had been cut with the ſithe, was "led" in "truſſes,"---or large bundles, each a horſe-load, bound together with two ropes, and laid acroſs a "pannel" or pad ſaddle, and ſteadied or "led" by a woman or youth, from the field. This was called "truſs leading" or "leading"---a term which is common at this time, in the North of England, and in Scotland, for carrying, hauling, or drawing hay, corn, or other article, on a carriage; and which, perhaps, owes its origin to an obſolete and forgotten practice, of a ſimilar nature, in thoſe Provinces.

In a general view, the Harveſt Management of this Diſtrict is below that of many others: nevertheleſs it differs, in various reſpects, from that of every other part of the kingdom; and certainly merits a place in a regiſter of the preſent ſtate of Engliſh Huſbandry.

The particularswhich require to be detailed are theſe:

I. HewingWheat, and Raking the Stubbles.

II. Setting up Shocks.

III. Making Arriſh Mows.

IV. Turning Corn in Swath.

V. Binding Oats and Barley out of Swath.

VI. CarryingSheaves on Horſeback.

VII. Pitching them to the Mow or Stack.

VIII. Form of Corn Stacks.

IX. Thatching Corn Stacks.

I. HEWING WHEAT. This is a kind of mowing with one hand. The "Yowing Hook" is formed much like the common ſharp-edged "hand reaping hook" of this and other places; but ſomewhat larger every way---longer, broader, and ſtouter; with a hooked knob at the end of the handle, to prevent its ſlipping out of the hand.

With this inſtrument, the corn is ſtruck at, horizontally, and almoſt cloſe to the ground,

ground, with the one hand; while the other hand and arm *ſtrike* it, at the ſame inſtant, about the middle of the ſtraw; thus driving it, upright, againſt the ſtanding corn: the workman taking a ſweep, round as much as will form a ſheaf, and collecting the whole together, in the center, into a ſort of leaning cone; finally ſtriking the hook under its baſe, to diſengage it entirely from the ſoil; but ſtill ſupporting it, with the left or looſe arm and the leg, until the hook be put beneath it, to lift it, horizontally, to the band.

In variation of this method, I have ſeen the hewer force his way up one ſide of a narrow ridge, againſt the wind, and back on the other ſide; thus collecting half a ſheaf; and then fetching another half ſheaf in the ſame manner.

This practice is not peculiar to the Weſt of England: it has long been in uſe, in the Southern Counties of Kent and Surrey: where, however, it is conſidered as a ſlovenly and bad practice. If a crop of wheat be free from weeds, and ſtand well upon its legs, this method of cutting is expeditious

expeditious and eligible enough: but, if the corn be lodged or ravelled, or foul at the bottom, with green ſucculent weeds, it is altogether improper: indeed, in the former caſe, it requires expert workmen to make good work.

A SITHE, in good hands, will make equal or better work, and is ſtill more expeditious.

To ſecure the ſcattered corn, which this looſe method of cutting leaves upon the ground, women or boys collect and ſet up the ſheaves; and are followed by women with RAKES, to draw together the looſe corn: GLEANING being ſeldom permitted, until the ſhocks be out of the fields *.

II. SHOCKS are here formed of ten ſheaves, ſet up in an extraordinary manner. Nine of them are crouded together in a ſquare, of three ſheaves every way, and

* Another diſtinguiſhing trait of the DEVONSHIRE HUSBANDRY is marked, by the HARVEST HOLLA,—which is here given when the *cutting of wheat* is finiſhed; and not, according to the ordinary cuſtom of England, when the laſt load of Corn is drawing home.

and the tenth is put over them, as a cloak or hood; the whole forming a ſort of cone or pyramid.

This is evidently a bad practice. The cloſe poſture of the ſheaves prevents a circulation of air among them; the center ſheaf being wholly excluded from it. And, in moſt caſes, the covering is very imperfect; one ſheaf, unleſs very large and the ſtraw very long, is not ſufficient to ſecure the reſt from rain water; but rather ſerves to conduct it into the centers of the upright ſheaves.

Shocks of ten ſheaves, with eight ſet up in a double row, and with two inverted as hoods or thatch, are much more ſecure and eligible. For the method of ſetting up Shocks of this deſcription, ſee MID. ECON. Vol. II. page 160.

III. "ARRISH MOWS"---or Field Stacklets. In a late harveſt, and in a moiſt climature, like that of Weſt Devonſhire and Cornwall, eſpecially after a wet ſummer, which ſeldom fails of filling the butts of corn ſheaves with green ſucculent herbage,

herbage,---ſecuring the ears from injury, and at the ſame time expoſing the butts to the influence of the atmoſphere, is, ſelf-evidently, an admirable expedient.

The ſize of Arriſh Mows varies. Thoſe which I have obſerved, generally contained about a waggon load of ſheaves. But they may be made of any ſize from a ſhock of ten ſheaves to a load.

The method of making them is this: a ſort of cone, or rather ſquare pyramid, being formed with ſheaves ſet upon their butts, and leaning towards the center, the workman gets upon them, on his knees; an aſſiſtant putting ſheaves, in their proper places, before him; while he crawls round the "mow;" *treading* them, in this manner, with his knees, applied about the banding place; and continuing thus to lay courſe after courſe, until the mow be deemed high enough: obſerving to contract the dimenſions as it riſes in height, and to ſet the ſheaves more and more upright, until they form, at the top, a ſharp point, ſimilar to that of nine ſheaves ſet up as a ſhock; and, like this, it is capped with an an inverted ſheaf, either of corn or of "reed:" the principle, and the form when finiſhed, being the ſame in both; namely, a ſquare pyramid: a form which would ſeem to have been taken from the pyramidal ſhock *.

Where corn is put up into theſe little ſtacks it is conſidered as ſafe, and is ſuffered to ſtand ſome weeks in them. I have ſeen ſheep feeding in the ſtubble, while the corn was ſtanding in theſe piles.

The only diſadvantage, perhaps, of this mode of harveſting, which is applicable to oats or barley as well as to wheat, is that of mice being thereby liable to be conveyed from the field to the barn.

IV. TURNING CORN SWATHS. This I have ſeen done BY HAND. The Corn, being gathered up carefully in the hands and arms, the turners face about, and ſpread it evenly upon freſh dry ground. This is an accurate mode of turning; and a good preparation for binding. But the turning

* Have not theſe practices been imported from the Continent?

turning of Corn Swaths is more generally done with ſlender poles, cut out of the hedges, ſix or eight feet long, about the ſize of a flail handle, and ſomewhat crooked: a tool which I have ſeen uſed in other Diſtricts. It is peculiarly well adapted to the purpoſe of *lifting* over Swaths; and ought to be everywhere in uſe *.

V. BINDING CORN SWATHS. In general, however, the Harveſting of mown Corn is done in a ſlovenly manner. The mowing is roughly performed, and the binding executed in a ſtill coarſer manner. In harveſting Oats, which had ſtood too long before they were cut, I have ſeen one fourth, if not one third, of the crop left ſhed upon the ground. In common practice, a very conſiderable ſhare of the crop is harveſted in the form of rakings; ſo much being left on the ground, after the ſheaves

* I have elſewhere aſſigned my reaſon for deſcending to the Minutiæ of the Harveſt Management. (See MID. ECON. Vol. II. p. 231.) The taſk of regiſtering the Manual Operations of Huſbandry is irkſome in the extreme. And nothing but a full conviction of its utility could induce me to perform it.

ſheaves are removed, that it requires to be raked *both ways*; namely, to be gone over twice; the ſecond raking being at right angles to the firſt.

In binding, the Swaths are rolled into "ſkoves," with ſhort rakes; the band ſtretched over the bundle; the ends, one in each hand, forced beneath it; the bundle lifted up, turned over, and the twiſted ends of the band tucked in.

If the crop be ſhort, "reed" is uſed for binding it: it was with the utmoſt difficulty I got a field of barley, which, through the thinneſs of the ſoil and the dryneſs of the ſummer, was too ſhort for bands, and which was clean, and in the higheſt order for ſtacking,---carried to the ſtack in waggons, without the expence and trouble of tying it up in bundles.

In a climate ſo uncertain as that of Weſt Devonſhire; and moſt eſpecially in a late harveſt; ſetting up mown corn in ſinglets, agreeably to the practice of the North of England, would, I am convinced, be the moſt eligible practice. For the method of ſetting up corn in this manner, ſee YORK. ECON. Vol. I. page 390

VI. In

VI. In CARRYING SHEAF CORN ON HORSEBACK, the Sheaves are packed in between the crooks, head to tail, with the butts outward, and carried up even; piling the load conſiderably above the horſe's back. The lower part of the load is laid in by hand, the upper part piled up with a fork; which being ſet firmly under one of the croſs bars of the crooks, a rope, previouſly thrown over, is pulled down tight and faſtened; the fork being a ſtay or purchaſe to pull againſt

A ſtring of horſes being thus laden, a boy travels them ſoberly to the barn or rick yard; where they are unloaded, by puſhing back the upper part of the load with the fork, throwing it over the tail of the horſe to the ground, or upon a cloth laid to receive it; the crooks being cleared, by hand, in a ſomewhat immechanical manner.

The whole ſtring unloaded, the boy mounts, and, ſtanding upright between the crooks, trots or perhaps gahops his horſes back to the field; frequently, to the no ſmall diſmay, or perhaps injury, of peaceful travellers. A ſomewhat uncivilized practice.

VII. PITCHING

VII. PITCHING CORN SHEAVES.

The Sheaves being thus left upon the floor or ground, without any advantage from a carriage, where the mow or ſtack riſes to a height above the reach of an ordinary fork, an expedient has been ſtruck out, and brought, by practice and the emulation of young men, to an extraordinary degree of ſlight and expertneſs. They are *flung*, provincially "pitched" from the point of a prong, formed very narrow in the tines, over the head of the pitcher; a boy placing the ſheaves fairly before him. I have ſeen a man thus PITCHING SHEAVES up to the roof of a ſtack above the ordinary height, throwing them ſeveral feet above the reach of his fork.

The ſpring is got by the arms and the knee jointly; or is done at arms length. When the height is very great, or the ſheaves heavy, two men's exertions, it ſeems, are joined: one man placing the tines of his pick under the "ſtem" or handle of the other! Much probably depends on the forming of the tines of the prong: they contract upwards to an acute angle: the

 ſheaves,

ſheaves, of courſe, part from them with a degree of ſpring, given by the ſtraw compreſſed between them.

VIII. The FORM OF STACKS. The ſtem is uſually carried up ſquare, and high; but the roof very flat, and hipped, or ſloped on every ſide: ſo that the roof, which in many Diſtricts contains nearly one third of the contents of the ſtack, does not here, perhaps, contain a ſixth of it. The difficulty of pitching from the ground, and the excellency of "reed" as a thatch, may have aſſiſted in fixing this prevailing faſhion.

IX. The METHOD OF THATCHING STACKS, in Weſt Devonſhire, is very judicious and effectual. The "reed" is ſpread thinly and evenly over the roof, and is faſtened with "ſpars" or hazel rods, pegged down to the butts of the ſheaves, and covered by the next courſe of reed, in the manner that reed roofs are laid, in Norfolk.

But, in Cornwall, I ſaw the reed faſtened

on

on with ſtraw ropes, ſtretched horizontally, within a few inches of each other; as in the Highlands of Scotland!

General Observations. Upon the whole, the buſineſs of Harveſt, except in as much as relates to the Field Management of mown Corn, and the forming of Wheat Shocks, may be ſaid to be well conducted, in this Diſtrict. It is true, that corn in general is here allowed leſs field room, or time between the cutting and the carrying, than it is in moſt other places; but, ſeeing the uncertainty of the climate, in this peninſular ſituation, the deviation is evidently on the right ſide.

13.

THE MANAGEMENT OF HARVESTED CROPS.

THE Homeſtall Management of this Country, varies ſo little from the ordinary practice of the Kingdom at large, as ſcarcely to require particular notice. There are, however, two or three peculiarities of Management which require to be regiſtered.

I. HOUSING STACKS BY HAND is not uncommon. Under the horſe-and-crook ſyſtem, it is perfectly eligible; and, where carriages are in uſe, it is comparatively more expeditious, than an East-countryman would readily allow. In an inſtance noticed, five men houſed about eight loads of wheat, in ſeven or eight hours. Two men, upon the ſtack, bound the ſheaves, in bundles of ten each, with ropes, and let them down, upon the ſhoulders of other two men, who carried them to the barn, from thirty to forty yards diſtance, and handed them up to the fifth man, on the mow. This piece of a ſtack would have broken deep into the day's work of a team; and, in a buſy time would have coſt twice the money the wages of theſe five men amounted to; which, at a ſhilling a day, was not more than three or four ſhillings.

II. The

II. The method of THRASHING WHEAT, in this Diſtrict, and throughout the Weſt of England, is too ſingular to be paſſed without notice. While ſtraw continues to be uſed as thatch, the practice is highly profitable.

The object of this method of Thraſhing (which is applicable to RYE, as well as to WHEAT), is to extract the grain from the ear, with the leaſt poſſible injury to the ſtraw. To this end, the ears are either thraſhed lightly with the flail, or they are beaten acroſs a caſk, by hand; until the grain be got pretty well out of them. If the corn is ſmutty, the latter is the more eligible method.

The next operation is to ſuſpend the ſtraw, in large double handfuls, in a ſhort rope, fixed high above the head, with an iron hook at the looſe end of it; which is put twice round the little ſheaflet, juſt below the ears, and faſtened with the hook's laying hold of the tight part of the rope. The left hand being now firmly placed upon the hook, and pulling downward, ſo as to twitch the ſtraw hard, and prevent the ears from ſlipping through it, the butts are freed from ſhort ſtraws and weeds, by means of a ſmall long-toothed rake or comb. This done, the rope is unhooked and the "reed" laid evenly in a heap.

A quantity of clean ſtraight unbruiſed ſtraw, or "reed," being thus obtained, it is formed into ſmall ſheaves, returned to the floor, and the ears thraſhed again with the flail, or is again thraſhed by hand over the caſk, to free it effectually from any remaining grain, which the former beating might have miſſed.

Laſtly, the reed is made up into large bundles — provincially "ſheaves"--- of 36 pound each; with all the ears at one end; the butts being repeatedly punched upon the floor, firſt in double handfuls, and then in the ſheaf, until they are as even, as if they had been cut off ſmooth and level, with a ſithe, or other long edgetool; while the ſtraws lie as ſtraight, and are almoſt as ſtout, as thoſe of inferior *reed*, or ſtems of the Arundo.

It is not for the purpoſe of thatch, only, that the ſtraw of wheat is carefully preſerved from

from the action of the flail; but for the purpose of litter also; it being found to last or wear much longer, in this capacity, than softly bruised straw; which may be said to be already on the road of decay, and to have passed the first stage toward the dunghill.

Women sometimes assist their husbands in the work of thrashing wheat, in this manner; as in beating it over the cask, or in raking out the loose straw, as well as in making up the reed *.

In thrashing BARLEY and OATS, the opened sheaves are piled on one side of the floor, and drawn over, heads-and-tails, to the other; the thrashers of the Western, as well as of the Northern extremity of the Kingdom, *keeping stroke*;---and, here, this

* In one instance, I saw a frame, for beating the ears over, instead of a cask; the construction somewhat resembling that of a very wide, short, crooked ladder, supported nearly horizontally, with its convex side upward; the cross bars being set edgeway, and a few inches from each other; and with an angular piece of wood running lengthway through the middle of the frame, and rising above the cross bars,—to separate, and spread with greater ease, the ears of the corn; and thereby to render the strokes the more effective.

animating practice is ſometimes extended to four thraſhers working in the ſame barn; performing a peal, which, though monotonous, is not diſpleaſing to the ear.

FODDER STRAW is here bound in very large, long, two-banded truſſes; no doubt that it may be the more eaſily "led" to the place where it is wanted. And where carriages are in uſe, the practice is continued.

III. The laſt particular of Practice, noticeable under the preſent head, is that of WINNOWING WITH THE NATURAL WIND. Farmers of every claſs (ſome few excepted) carry their corn into the field, on horſeback, perhaps a quarter of a mile, from the barn, to the ſummit of ſome airy ſwell; where it is winnowed, *by women!* the miſtreſs of the farm, perhaps, being expoſed, in the ſevereſt weather, to the cutting winds of winter, in this ſlaviſh, and truly barbarous employment. The obſolete practice of the Northern extremity of the Iſland, in which farmers loaded their wives and daughters with dung, to be carried to the fields on their backs, was but a little a little more uncivilized. The machine fan, however, is at length, making its way into the Weſtern extremity.

14.

MARKETS.

PLYMOUTH, and its environs, form the metropolis of the Diſtrict, in which its various products may be ſaid to concenter. The conſumption, there, depends much however upon the circumſtances of War and Peace.

TAVISTOCK, neverthelefs, has a good CORN MARKET: a large flour mill, in this place, is conducted with judgement and ſpirit.

The STOCK FAIRS of the Diſtrict are chiefly thoſe of Taviſtock; where very great numbers of lean cattle, bred in Cornwall and Weſt Devonſhire, are bought up, by by Somersetshire and other East-country Graziers. There are, however, several VILLAGE FAIRS, in this, as in other parts of the Island.

15.

WHEAT,

AND ITS

PARTICULAR MANAGEMENT.

IN registering the minutial Management of this and the other crops of the District, I shall follow the same Plan of Arrangement, as I have, on every other occasion, found it right to pursue.

I. The SPECIES of Wheat usually cultivated is the common white Wheat.

II. SUCCESSION. It is universally sown on ley ground.

III. SOIL. It is grown on every sort.

IV. The

IV. The SOIL PROCESS is moſtly that which has been deſcribed, under the general head, MANAGEMENT OF THE SOIL; namely, that of cutting or tearing off the ſod, and burning it. But this is not invariably the practice: ſometimes the Ley is broken up by a full depth plowing; which, I think, is called "rotting the ſpine." To this ſucceeds a ſort of rough baſtard fallow; the roots and rubbiſh, which harrow up, being burnt, if the weather be ſavorable.

V. MANURE. Formerly, SEA SAND and DUNG were in uſe. Now chiefly LIME, with perhaps a ſmall portion of dung. The METHOD of LIMING has been deſcribed. See page 158.

VI. SEED PROCESS. This is one of the many operations, belonging to the eſtabliſhed practice of the Diſtrict under ſurvey, which have ſo little reſemblance to the eſtabliſhed practice of the Iſland at large, that they can ſcarcely be conſidered as belonging to Britiſh huſbandry.

A mere Provincialiſt of the central, or the

the Northern parts of the Iſland, might travel through all the countries of Europe, and not find practices leſs foreign to his own, than thoſe of Devonſhire.

The TIME OF SOWING Wheat is late; the ſeed time continuing from October to near Chriſtmas. The reaſon given for late ſowing is, that "early ſown crops are liable to weeds." This precaution, added to the burning and the lime (as before mentioned), account more fully for the cleanneſs of the Wheat crops of this Diſtrict, notwithſtanding the foulneſs of the ſoil with reſpect to weed ſeeds. But in a backward and uncertain climature, late ſowing cannot be altogether right.

The SEED PLOWING, which, in the ordinary practice of the Diſtrict, is the only full-depth plowing given for Wheat, takes place immediately previous to the ſowing. The ſoil is, I believe, invariably, laid up in narrow lands; and, in general, diagonally acroſs the field! The uſual width is four bouts, or eight plits; one plit, or narrow balk, being left ſtanding in each interfurrow.

Pre-

Previous to the ſowing, the entire ſurface of the field is HACKED OVER, BY HAND! with large heavy hoes or hacks: each man taking two plits; which, in the ſeed plowing for Wheat, are plowed of a narrow width, and which, in this operation, are cut into ſquare clods, the ſize of ſpits or ſpade bits: and, it is very probable, the practice has grown out of the hand culture, which, in every country, probably, preceded the uſe of the plow.

The QUANTITY OF SEED from two to two and a half Wincheſter buſhels.

SOWN in ſeparate ridges, and at one caſt.

COVERED, with light harrows and two horſes.

ADJUSTED, in an extraordinary manner. Until very lately, the interfurrows were univerſally hacked and ſhovelled out, *by hand*. The unplowed ſlips, having been reduced to fragments with hacks, were thrown over the ridges, or into hollows or vacancies, by the ſides of the furrows, and the ſurface otherwiſe adjuſted, with ſhovels. Now, it is become the more general practice, to open the furrows with the plow; a

double

double mouldboard plow being uſed by ſome farmers. The rows or ridgets of ſoil and clods, forced up by the plow, on either ſide of the furrow, are afterwards pulled upward, and the ſurface in general adjuſted, with "haul-to's"—or three-tined dung drags; giving the ridges, with this rude tool, a degree of finiſh.

General observations. It need not be remarked, that the ſetting about, and the ſpreading of lime and earth,—hacking over the ridges, and finally adjuſting them, require a great ſupply of hand labour. Ten acres of Wheat put into the ground, in the manner of this Diſtrict, take up more manual labor, than fifty acres ſown in the ordinary way. Nevertheleſs, the labor is not all loſt; the land, beſide receiving additional tilth in the operation, is more evenly ſeeded, and with a leſs quantity of ſeed, than it would require without it; and, in a country where labor is plentiful and cheap, it might be wrong to withhold any part of it, ſo long as the preſent ſyſtem of management ſhall be purſued.

The

The other operations, reſpecting the culture of Wheat, are ſufficiently explained, under the GENERAL HEADS.

VII. The PRODUCE OF WHEAT, by *the ſtatute acre*, is eſtimated at twenty Wincheſter buſhels.

16.

BARLEY,

AND ITS

MANAGEMENT.

AFTER what has been ſaid, in deſcribing the GENERAL OPERATIONS of the ARABLE MANAGEMENT, little remains to be added, here.

I. The SPECIES of Barley grown is chiefly, or wholly, the common LONG

EARED

EARED kind. Other ſorts, it ſeems, have been tried; but have been given up for this.

II. The SUCCESSION. Barley ſucceeds WHEAT, or TURNEPS, or ſometimes BARLEY itſelf: the laſt of the three grain crops, which the preſent ſyſtem of aration *requires*, being in this caſe Barley, inſtead of Oats.

III. The SOIL. Barley is grown on all the better lands; which, indeed, are the beſt adapted to this grain. On the thinner ſoils, towards the Moorſides, Oats are more generally cultivated.

IV. TILLAGE for Barley. After Wheat, two plowings, or rather one plowing and a half: after Turneps, one plowing; the charlock and other weeds being previouſly burnt!

V. MANURE. Seldom any uſed, I believe, for Barley.

VI. SOW-

VI. SOWING. TIME OF SOWING—April. QUANTITY OF SEED—four buſhels and upward! METHOD OF SOWING—broadcaſt, above.

VII. WEEDING. Univerſally, I believe, hand-weeded.

For HARVESTING, THRASHING, &c. ſee the GENERAL HEADS.

PRODUCE of Barley—from thirty to forty buſhels an acre. It is, of courſe, a profitable crop; and ought frequently to be grown on lands, which are *forced* to produce Wheat.

17.

OATS.

THE SPECIES moſtly black; as being leſs liable to be diſcoloured in this moiſt dirty climate. TILLAGE, one plowing. TIME OF SOWING, February and March.

QUANTITY OF SEED, five or ſix buſhels.

PRODUCE, not regiſtered.

Indeed, the culture of this crop being in a conſiderable degree confined to the Moorſide farms, I paid the leſs attention to its culture.

18.

TURNEPS.

NOTWITHSTANDING the unhuſbandlike manner, in which Turneps are ſtill cultivated, in this Diſtrict, it is more than half a century ſince they were introduced into field culture:—a ſtrong evidence of the ſupineneſs of the Devonſhire huſbandmen.

I. The SPECIES, various; but not excellent. The proper method of raiſing the ſeed

ſeed does not appear to be underſtood, or is not attended to *.

II. SUCCESSION. Turneps are invariably ſown on graſs land. There never, perhaps, had been an acre of turneps grown in the Diſtrict, after a grain crop, until I introduced the practice. Some account of the attendant circumſtances will appear, in the MINUTES.

III. TILLAGE, &c. for Turneps, is the ſame as for Wheat. Namely, velling or ſkirting; burning; and one plowing.

IV. For MANURE, the BEAT ASHES are chiefly depended upon; and without them, it has been believed, no Turneps could be grown.

V. The SOWING is done chiefly, in July. The QUANTITY OF SEED, one to two pints.

 VI. The

* For the Norfolk practice, in raiſing Turnep ſeed, ſee NORF. ECON. Vol. I. P. 278.

VI. The HOING of Turneps has not yet found its way into the ordinary practice of the District. In Autumn, the Turnep grounds are as yellow, as Mustard Fields in May; and, in winter, as white with the opened pods of the Charlock, as stubbles in Autumn: the silvery pods and withered branches of the weeds, shading and nearly hiding the green tops of the Turneps: not in the immediate District of the station only; but in other parts of the County. This phenomenon struck me most forcibly in travelling between Exeter and Plymouth, in the latter end of December 1791.

Many individuals, it is true, attempt to draw the weeds, by hand; piling them in heaps, upon the ground. But the whole crop, I apprehend, is rarely if ever got through, in this way. And what is done, is probably done at a much greater expence, than hoing would have incurred.

VII. The EXPENDITURE of Turneps is judicious. They are chiefly drawn, and thrown upon ley grounds, to cattle and

and ſheep; or carried to ſtalls, for fatting cattle; agreeably to the Norfolk practice!

GENERAL OBSERVATION ON THE TURNEP CULTURE.

It is not fitting, nor likely, that this part of the Iſland, alone, ſhould remain much longer a diſgrace to Britiſh Agriculture, in reſpect to the culture of this valuable crop. And yet, if I may judge from my own experience, the hand hoing of Turneps cannot readily be introduced. For although, by perſonal attention, I ſucceeded equally to my expectation; yet, whenever that attention was called off, a relaxation or neglect of the operation took place: ſo rooted, and difficult to eradicate, is the cuſtom of half a century.

If I were to venture to recommend any practice, to the Gentlemen who are now evincing a deſire of rouſing their countrymen to a ſenſe of their delinquency, it would be to change, entirely, the preſent mode of raiſing Turneps; and to adopt that which has been lately ſtruck out, in the South of

Scotland, and which is now making its way, very rapidly, into the North of England: namely, that of ſowing them on narrow ridges, ſimilar to thoſe in which potatoes are ſometimes raiſed, in the Diſtrict under view: a method that appears to me ſingularly adapted to the ſhallower ſoils of Devonſhire; which, in general, are well ſuited to the Turnep culture.

19.

POTATOES.

THE HISTORY of the Potatoe crop, as an object of field culture, in this Weſtern Diſtrict, furniſhes another inſtance of the reſpect which its cultivators have long borne to eſtabliſhed cuſtoms. It is not more than twentyfive years, if ſo much, ſince the entire Country, including, I believe, the markets of Plymouth, was ſupplied with Potatoes from the neighbourhood

hood of Morton Hampſtead, at the oppoſite end of Dartmore, and at not leſs than twenty miles diſtance from the center of this Diſtrict, nor leſs than thirty miles from Plymouth and its dock yard! The film of prejudice, however, being at length ſeen through, Potatoes were found to grow, and to produce their kind, at the Weſt end, as well as at the Eaſt end, of Dartmore; and, now, the Diſtrict raiſes enough to furniſh its own conſumption, and to ſupply the markets in its neighbourhood; though the population, probably, has much encreaſed, during the lapſe of five and twenty years.

It is reaſonable to ſuppoſe that the people of Morton, while they monopolized, and practiſed as a myſtery, the culture of Potatoes, during a length of time, would not be inattentive to the minutiæ of cultivation; and it is equally probable, that the knowledge they acquired travelled Weſtward, with the operation. Let this be as it may, the culture of Potatoes is, at preſent, well underſtood, here; and, in one particular, at leaſt, deſerves to be copied.

I. The SPECIES of Potatoes, here as in moſt other places, are various; not only in ſhape, colour, and farinaceous quality, but in the nature of their growth; the different ſorts requiring different times of planting: a circumſtance which is not, perhaps, ſufficiently attended to, in other Diſtricts.

II. SUCCESSION. Potatoes ſucceed, invariably I believe, Ley herbage;—broken, ſometimes at leaſt, by two or three PLOWINGS; but no BURNING is uſed for this crop.

III. PLANTING. TIME OF PLANTING—March, April, May, or even June; according to the varieties or ſorts which are cultivated: it being found that each has its favorite ſeaſon of planting: and it is probable that, were attention paid to the varieties of every other Diſtrict, ſimilar propenſities might be diſcovered.

The METHOD OF PLANTING varies. Sometimes they are planted in alternate furrows, and covered with DUNG. In other inſtances, they are planted in ſlips or beds;

beds; narrow ridges of mold being left between them, to earth up the plants, in the lazy-bed way.

IV. The CLEANING of Potatoes is well attended to. They are hoed; and I have seen those planted in alternate furrows, earthed up, in a husbandlike manner.

V. VI. Potatoes are TAKEN UP, in November, and December; and PRESERVED in pits.

VII. The FARM EXPENDITURE of Potatoes is chiefly, or wholly, on Swine. And, from the restrictive clause in Leases, see page 80, it is probable that even this is a modern mode of expenditure.

20.

CULTIVATED HERBAGE.

IT has been already mentioned, that the cultivation of herbage is of more than half a century ſtanding, in the Diſtrict under ſurvey. From this circumſtance, and from the cultivation of Turneps, and the uſe of Lime as a manure, having been introduced about the ſame time, it would ſeem that, about ſixty years ago, a STAGE OF IMPROVEMENT took place; ſince which time the practice appears to have been ſtationary; and it is, of courſe, now fully prepared for another ſtep.

The PROPORTIONAL QUANTITY OF LEY, in the incloſed country, is full two thirds of the arable lands, or lands occaſionally plowed, conſidered as diſtinct from meadows, grazing grounds, and rough upland

land paſtures. But, on the ſkirts of the moors and commons, which ſerve as ſummer paſtures, the proportion is much leſs.

I. The SPECIES of herbage which is here cultivated are chiefly RED CLOVER and RAYGRASS—provincially "Eaver:" but WHITE CLOVER, and TREFOIL, are occaſionally ſown.

II. SUCCESSION. In the ordinary practice of the country, cultivated herbage ſucceeds Oats, after Barley, after Wheat! A practice which we have ſeen, bad as it is, *enforced* by reſtrictive clauſes in a modern leaſe.

III. SOWING. The uſual TIME is between the ſowing of the corn and its coming up. The QUANTITY OF SEED 12lb. of Clover, and half a buſhel of Raygraſs.

IV. APPLICATION. Mown the firſt year: afterwards paſtured.

V. DURATION. Six or ſeven years, in the incloſed country; leſs, by the ſides of the commons.

21.

GRASSLANDS,

AND THEIR

MANAGEMENT.

I. SPECIES OF GRASSLANDS

THE GRASSLANDS of this Diſtrict may be claſſed under

1. MEADOW LANDS, or cool and frequently rich bottoms, or dips; as well as more upland ſites, over which water can be ſpread; and which are kept in a ſtate of MOWING GROUND *.

2. GRA-

* MEADOW PLANTS. I collected moſt of them; but not with ſufficient accuracy, as to their proportional quantity, to entitle the liſt to publication.

The

2. GRAZING GROUNDS, or rich uplands, over which water has not been conducted; and which are kept in a ſtate of PASTURAGE.

3. The TEMPORARY LEYS, juſt mentioned; which are uſed as MOWING GROUND, the firſt year; and afterward, as PASTURE GROUNDS. And

4. ROUGH UPLANDS, which ſometimes, though not frequently, occur on private property, and are kept in a ſtate of coarſe PASTURAGE.

II. MANAGEMENT OF GRASS-LANDS. In the managemen of PASTURE

The ſpecies, found in the meadows of Buckland Place, are the ordinary ſpecies of meadow lands, in moſt parts of the Iſland; with, however, one remarkable difference: the meadow Foxtail (*Alopecurus pratenſis*) is wanting!

The late accurate Botaniſt, and amiable man, Mr. HUDSON (Author of FLORA ANGLICA) had ſome ſeeds of this Plant collected, in the neighbourhood of London (at the requeſt of our mutual friend the late SIR FRANCIS DRAKE), and ſown over theſe meadows; but without ſucceſs. In the ſummer of 1794, I examined, with ſome attention, the part over which they were ſown; but could not diſcover that any of them had taken root.

TURE GROUNDS, I met with nothing noticeable; except the extraordinary foulneſs of many of the Leys; which has been already noticed, under the head—MANAGEMENT OF THE SOIL. I ſhall therefore confine my remarks, under this head, to MOWING GROUNDS, and more particularly, to

WATERED MEADOWS. The *origin* of the practice of watering Graſslands, artificially, in this Diſtrict, cannot be reached by memory; nor does tradition, I believe, attempt to aſcertain it. There is a ſtriking inſtance of the antiquity of the practice obſervable, on the farm of Buckland Priory. A hedge, in appearance ſome centuries old, winds by the ſide of a water courſe, evidently formed by art, for the purpoſe of conveying a rill, along the brow of a ſwell of rich Graſsland, which bears no mark of having ever been in a ſtate of aration. From the winding direction, and the regular deſcent, or almoſt levelneſs, of this artificial rill, there is every reaſon to believe, that it was formed prior to the Hedge; which may ſeem to have ſince been run along the upperſide of it. From the circumſtance of this

this farm having been monaſtic, one is led to conclude that the practice was introduced under the auſpices of the Church: or, if we go ſtill farther back, we may conjecture that it was brought over by the firſt ſettlers, or by future Coloniſts, from the South of Europe; where it has been, for ages paſt, in uſe.

But this by the way: Hiſtory, eccleſiaſtic or profane, may perhaps furniſh thoſe, who have leiſure to look for them, with better lights.

The *quantity* of watered lands, in this Diſtrict, is, in ſome townſhips, conſiderable; while, in others, where the vallies are narrow, and their ſides wooded, little watered ground is ſeen. There remains, however, much to be done in this reſpect. Perhaps, not half the quantity of the lands, capable of receiving this admirable improvement, enjoy it at preſent; and

The *management* of thoſe which are ſubjected to the practice, whatever it may have been heretofore, is, at preſent, far from being accurate. The ſoil is imperfectly drained, and the water imperfectly ſpread over

over it. Presently before my going down into the District, a person of the first practice in it had been employed, to conduct the water over the meadows of Buckland Place; which had previously lain in a state of neglect. Nevertheless, I found them still in such a state, as induced me to have the whole laid out, afresh, under my own directions.

Yet, the *effect of the water*, notwithstanding the low ebb at which the watering of lands is found; at this day, is such as I have no where observed; except in the neighbourhood of chalk hills. It gives a greenness and grossness of herbage, nearly equal to that of the meadows of Wiltshire and Hampshire.

This led me to conceive that the slatey rock, out of which the most efficacious of these waters filter. contained some considerable proportion of calcareous matter. But, from the experiments already mentioned, the proportionate quantity of calcareous earth, contained in these slate rocks, appears to be small.

Nevertheless, it might be dangerous to con-

conclude, from this, that the waters under consideration do not contain a sufficient quantity of the calcareous principle, to enable them to produce the effect which we are desirous to account for. Indeed, it is not a knowledge of the component parts of the filtering stratum, but of those of the waters themselves, which is most desirable.

ACCURATE ANALYSES of WATERS, whose effects are *known*, as MANURES, are very much to be desired. That different waters are as various, in their effects on vegetation, as distinct vegetable and animal substances are, must be evident to every one who has made extensive observations on these effects. And CHEMISTRY cannot bestow on AGRICULTURE more valuable assistance, than in prosecuting enquiries of this nature.

The HAY HARVEST of West Devonshire has little to recommend it, as a pattern to other Districts.

The *mowing* is, in general, ill done. The sithe is short, and laid in, too near the handle. The unavoidable consequence is, the work goes on slowly, or a line of uncut herbage is left between each ſtroke. I have ſeen worſe mowing, both of graſs and corn, in this Diſtrict, than in any other. This cenſure, however, does not apply to the country in general. I have alſo ſeen good work in it.

The *Hay-making* of the Diſtrict ſtands in a ſimilar predicament. Some I have ſeen vilely managed; others conducted on the beſt principles of the art: namely, ſpread, turned, cocked in ſmall cocks, reſpread, turned, recocked, or carried.

But, in theſe operations, a principal tool, the PRONG, is ridiculouſly too ſmall; fitter for the hands of a Cook, than a Haymaker: the tines, even of thoſe uſed for loading carriages, are not longer than thoſe of a Man of War's beef-fork. But they were faſhioned under the Horſe and Crook huſbandry, and when carriages are uſed, they ſtill remain unchanged.

The *carrying of Hay in crooks* I have ſeen done in a neat and ſecure manner. The ends or faces of the load are carried up ſtraight, and appear in folds, like thoſe formed at the corners of waggon loads, in ſome

ſome Diſtricts. This gives firmneſs to the load, and prevents its being ſcattered by the way.

The AFTERGRASS of meadows is, here, judiciouſly managed: it is ſuffered to grow to a full bite, but not to be overgrown, before ſtock be turned upon it.

I have ſeen cattle put into a meadow immediately after the Hay was got out of it, "to pick about the hedges:"—an accurate minutia of management. For the herbage, which is then ſucculent and edible to ſtore cattle, would, before the aftergraſs were ready to be paſtured off, become unpalatable, and be altogether neglected by cows or fatting ſtock, with freſh ſucculent herbage before them. It would be evidently wrong, however, to ſuffer ſuch cattle to remain in freſh mown grounds, after they have performed the principal intention.

See MID. ECON. Vol. II. P. 130. on this ſubject.

 22. THE

22.

THE MANAGEMENT OF ORCHARDS AND FRUIT LIQUOR IN *WEST DEVONSHIRE, &c.*

AFTER the ample detail already given of the management of Orchards and Fruit Liquor in HEREFORDSHIRE, &c. * little may ſeem to be requiſite, on the preſent occaſion. But when, on examination, we find the practices of the two Diſtricts, eſpecially with reſpect to Orchards, ſo widely different, as to appear pretty evidently to have had ſeparate origins, the propriety of regiſtering the management of Devonſhire, in detail, will be readily admitted.

In

* See GLO. ECON. Vol. II. p. 239.

In examining the practice of this District, I find it requisite to follow nearly the same steps which I took in going over that of Herefordshire; and to examine

First, Orchards.

Second, Fruit Liquor.

I. ORCHARDS. The particulars which present themselves, on viewing this branch of the subject, in the present case, are

1. The introduction of Orchards into the District.
2. The quantity of Orchard grounds it contains.
3. Species of Orchard fruits.
4. The situation of Orchards.
5. The soils of Orchards.
6. The method of raising Orchard trees.
7. Planting Orchard trees.
8. Aftermanagement of Orchards.
9. The application of the ground of Orchards.

1. The first INTRODUCTION of Orchards, into this District, appears to be pretty well ascertained. One of the Or-

chards of Buckland Priory is ſaid to be the oldeſt in the country, and this is ſpoken of as being about two hundred years old.

Nevertheleſs, this Orchard is ſtill fully ſtocked, and in full bearing! A fact which the Orchardmen of Herefordſhire will not readily credit. A fact, however, which is perfectly reconcileable, when the practice of this Diſtrict is explained *.

2. The AGGREGATE QUANTITY of Orchard ground, in this Diſtrict, is conſiderable. For though the Orchards in general are ſmall, compared with thoſe of Herefordſhire, &c.; yet the Farms being alſo ſmall, and each having its Orchard, the number is of courſe great. Nevertheleſs, the proportional quantity of Orchard grounds to culturable lands, is much leſs, here, than in the Mayhill Diſtrict †.

3. The

* This particular, with many others relating to the preſent ſubject, I had from Mr. STAPLETON of MONK'S BUCKLAND; who may, I believe, be ſaid to have a more accurate knowledge of the management of Orchards and Cider, than any other man in the country.

† ORCHARDS OF CORNWALL. The Cider country, I am well informed, does not reach more than half the length

3. The SPECIES of FRUIT is invariably the APPLE, when Liquor is the object *.

For the Fruit markets, *Cherries*, *Pears*, and *Walnuts*, are raiſed in great abundance; eſpecially in the townſhip of Beer Ferries; which is ſaid to ſend out of it a thouſand pounds worth of fruit (including Strawberries) annually.

4. The SITUATIONS of Orchards are chiefly in vallies, and dips or hollows, near houſes; not ſpread over the arable land, and paſture grounds, as in Herefordſhire and Gloceſterſhire. Neverthleſs, there are grounds, not only well adapted for arable crops, but for water meadows, which are at preſent appropriated to Orchards. On the Barton of Buckland there are twenty or thirty acres of land of the laſt deſcrip-

P 4 tion,

length of the county. Below that, the ſea air is injurious to Orchards; the land growing narrower, and there being fewer vallies to ſhelter them, in the Weſtern extremity of the county, than there are in the Eaſtern parts, and in Devonſhire.

* The ſoil, perhaps, is not adapted to the PEAR TREE, which affects a cool ſtrong ſoil. See GLO. ECON. Vol. II. P. 263.

tion, encumbered with Orchard trees, which have never paid for planting and land room; and which ought forthwith to be diſorcharded; and there are other Orchard grounds in the ſame predicament, on different parts of this Eſtate: not ariſing ſo much, perhaps, from *locality*, as from *aſpect*.

Part of the Orchards, here under notice, lie bleakly expoſed to the North: part in the opening of a deep valley, in the current of the Southweſt wind.

Much of the ſucceſs of Orchards depends on ſituation. The Orchards which ſucceed beſt, in this Diſtrict, are ſituated in dips or hollows, which are neither expoſed to the bleak blaſts from the North Eaſt, nor to the *ſea winds*, from the Weſt and Southweſt. Deep narrow vallies, whoſe ſides are precipitous, and neither fit for corn nor meadow, and which are not liable to the winds here noticed, as they blow acroſs them, are ſingularly eligible for Orchard grounds; and there are many ſuch, probably, which have not yet been planted. While, it is equally probable, much of the ground,

ground, at preſent in a ſtate of Orchard, might be converted to a better purpoſe.

5. Soils. The richeſt deepeſt ſoils appear to have been choſen for Orchard grounds. It is probable that the ſhallower ſoils of this Diſtrict are unfit for fruit trees; but, where ſituation will admit, ſuch as are encumbered with large ſtones, with good intervening ſoil, are ſingularly eligible; and, in ſome caſes, I have ſeen them choſen.

6. Plants for Orchards are raised, either by nurſerymen; or by farmers, for their own and their neighbours' uſe; or by cottagers for ſale; or by landlords to ſupply their tenants.

In the management of nurſery plants, the moſt remarkable circumſtance is that of *training* them, with ſtems, not more than three or four feet high! A practice which is ſo different from that of other fruit-liquor countries; indeed, from that of every part of this Iſland, Devonſhire and Cornwall excepted; a ſtranger is inclined to condemn it, at firſt ſight, as being guided by ignorance or folly of the loweſt claſs.

Whether it has been adopted, originally, to

to avoid the ill effect of the winds, or to bring the fruitbearing wood near the ground, and thereby to gain a more genial atmosphere, for the fruit to mature in; or whether it may have arisen out of the practice of gathering crab stocks in the woods, and rough grounds, where they frequently take a low shrubby form, may now be difficult to ascertain: at present, the practice appears to be followed, merely, as an established custom.

The disadvantages of low fruit trees will be mentioned, in speaking of the *Application of the Land* of Orchards.

7. In the PLANTING of Fruit Trees, the Orchardmen of West Devonshire excel. A stronger proof of this need not be produced, than the circumstance of their keeping the same ground in a state of orchard, in perpetuity. As the old trees go off, young ones are planted, in the interspaces, without any apprehensions of miscarriage.

In *setting out* Orchards, the practice of Devonshire is not less *unique*, than it is in training the plants. A statute rod, namely five ſive yards and a half, may be taken as the ordinary *diſtance* between the plants! Some I have meaſured at not more than four yards apart: ſome few at ſix yards.

The moſt approved *mode of planting* is to remove the ſoil down to the rock, which ſeldom lies very deep, and to cover this, eight or ten inches thick, with a compoſt of freſh earth and ſea ſand. Upon this compoſt, in ordinary caſes, the inverted turf is laid; and upon this the young tree is ſet; and its roots bedded in the beſt of the excavated mold; finally covering them with the ordinary earth raiſed in making the pit. A method which is altogether judicious.

The uſual *guard* are faggots of brambles, bruſhwood, or furze; letting them remain to rot at the foot of the tree. No ſtakes, I believe, are uſed. Indeed, the plants are generally ſo low as not to require them: eſpecially in *filling up old Orchards*; as the old trees ſhelter the young ones from the wind. And the *planting of new Orchards* does not appear to be, at preſent, much in practice.

practice. I have not obſerved it, in more than one or two inſtances.

8. The AFTERMANAGEMENT of Orchards is confined to ſupplying the trees with freſh brambles, furze, and frith—ſtraw and weeds---to rot on their roots: not over the paſture of the feeding fibers, but round the ſtem (in ſuch a manner however as not to touch it). Yet it is believed, by men who pay attention to theſe matters, that the growth and fruitfulneſs of the trees are much promoted through theſe means. Does the dead matter, by deſtroying the living herbage, become the means of a ſupply of air to the larger roots, and thus aſſiſt the ſap in its aſcent? The popular idea is, that theſe ſubſtances "find their way down to the roots" *

It will not be improper to relate, that I have heard the *canker* (the great enemy of modern Orchards) ſet at naught! Not, however, by a man on whoſe judgement I have a ſufficient reliance, to become a voucher

* For an inſtance of INVERTING THE SWARD of an Orchard, by way of meliorating the Trees, ſee the MINUTES.

voucher for the truth of his opinions. "A zeam of zand" applied to the root is an infallible remedy. "Common river ſand, or the ſand of Rooborough Down will do." The canker, he believes, is owing to too much "dreſſing," or additional ſubſtances applied to the roots; or to too great richneſs of ſoil, which he thinks the ſand corrects or qualifies.

I regiſter theſe ideas the rather, as they accord with my own theory of the canker: and in evidence of the truth of the theory, and the juſtneſs of the practice, the true Redſtreak, or an apple, which, as well as the tree that bears it, reſembles the Herefordſhire Redſtreak, formerly of ſo much celebrity, is ſtill cultivated, here, with great eaſe and certainty *.

The *pruning* of Fruit Trees, appears to be little attended to; after they are planted in the Orchard.

With reſpect to the *cleaning* of Fruit Trees, I have neither ſeen, nor heard, of any traces of ſuch a practice. During the winter months, a Weſt Devonſhire Orchard, by

* But ſee forward.

by reaſon of the lowneſs of the trees, perhaps, and the humidity of the climate, appears as if hung with hoar froſt; owing to the *white moſs* which hangs in ribbons from its boughs. The *Miſleto* is not known to this Diſtrict, nor I believe, to any part of Devonſhire or Cornwall.

9. The APPLICATION OF THE LAND of Orchards. Here lies the great objection to the Devonſhire Orchard. The uſe of the land is in a great meaſure thrown away. Horſes are ſuffered to run through them, in winter, and calves are kept in them, in early ſpring; but grown cattle and ſheep are, at all times, prohibited from entering: while fruit is on the trees, the very ſwine are carefully kept out of them; even ſmall pigs; leſt they ſhould gather the fruit as it hangs on the boughs! which, in a bearing year, bend to the ground, and perhaps reſt upon it; while weeds, three or four feet high, ſhoot up among them, and, of courſe, overſhadow the fruit.

Previous to the gathering ſeaſon, the weeds are cut down with the ſithe, and thrown to the roots of the trees; that the fruit

fruit may be found: an operation, however, which is too often neglected until the first windfalls have rotted on the ground; and a double destruction of hog food has taken place *.

II. FRUIT LIQUOR. Where the consumption of any article lies chiefly within the District of Manufacture, there is the less stimulus to excellency of management, than where a common market creates an emulation among those who supply it. From the Southern Parts of Devonshire, more or less Cider is sent to the London market; but very little from this Western District. Nevertheless, I have tasted Cider of a superior

* An idea prevails, here, that apples are not nutritious to hogs. It is very probable that apples, alone, would not be so; but considering the nature of the hog, with respect to the heat and dryness of his habit, and the well known effect of acidulating his beverage; and seeing the avidity with which he devours fruit of every kind;—it is more than probable, that suffering swine to pick up the early windfall fruit, previous to the first grinding, is much more eligible than letting it waste among the weeds and grass; which, if likewise thrown open to store swine, would have been a farther source of profit to their owners.

perior quality, made in West Devonshire. Indeed, its climature, in a moderately dry summer, seems to be much better adapted to the production of this species of Fruit Liquor, than is that of Herefordshire or Glocestershire.

In taking a view of the West Devonshire practice, it will be proper to examine, separately, the following particulars.

1. The Manufactory.
2. The Fruit.
3. Breaking.
4. Pressing.
5. The Must.
6. Fermenting.
7. The Liquor.
8. Produce.
9. Markets.

1. The ordinary PLACE OF MANUFACTURE, provincially the "POUND HOUSE,"—is generally a mean shed or hovel, without peculiarity of form, or any trace of contrivance. On the larger Bartons, or where the Orchard grounds are extensive, appropriate buildings are fitted up, in different ways. The

The only pound houſe, I examined, which has any claim to merit, in reſpect to *plan*, is that of MR. STAPLETON of MONKS BUCKLAND; which, though not on a large ſcale, is perhaps, in the arrangement or general economy of its more eſſential parts, as near perfection, as the nature of a Fruit Liquor Manufactory will admit of, or requires.

The building is a long ſquare, ſtanding *acroſs* a gentle deſcent. Behind it is a platform or flooring of looſe ſtones, (the rubbiſh of a ſlate quarry) to receive the fruit, as it is gathered, and to give it the firſt ſtage of maturation, in the open air. The ground floor, of one end of the building, contains the mill and preſs. Over this part, is a loft or chamber, in which the apples receive the laſt ſtage of maturation, and from which they are conveyed, by a ſpout, into the mill. The ground floor of the other end of the building is the fermenting room, ſunk a few ſteps below the floor of the mill and preſs room; a pipe or ſhoot conveying the liquor, from the preſs, into a ciſtern in the fermenting room.

Thus far, the plan may be ſaid to be compleat. If, over the fermenting room, an empty caſk loft were fitted up; and, on a ſtage below it, a keeping room or ſtore cellar were ſet apart for the fermented liquor: and, further, if a contiguous room, fitted up with a boiler, were made to communicate, equally, with the fermenting room, and the empty caſk room, for the conveniency of coopering and ſcalding the caſks, ſuch premiſes might be ſaid to be compleat in all their parts.

On principles ſimilar to thoſe which are here ſuggeſted, I made ſuch alterations in the cider rooms of Buckland Place, as the ſituation of the buildings would admit of, without great expence. They are on the largeſt ſcale of any I have ſeen; and are probably, in many reſpects, the firſt ſuite of *private* cider rooms, in the kingdom.

2. FRUIT. The *ſpecies*, as has been ſaid, is ſolely the APPLE, whoſe *varieties* are, here, numerous; though not ſo endleſs, as they are in Herefordſhire; the propagation of *kernel fruits* being leſs frequent, in this Diſtrict. Many of the ſorts are of

an

an old ſtanding. The Golden Pipin, however, is going off; "it cankers and will not take;" ſo that the identity of the Redſtreak may be doubted. See above, page 221.

In the *gathering* of fruit, there is nothing either excellent or peculiar; except in the circumſtance of fruit being gathered wet or dry: a circumſtance which may have ariſen out of the moiſtneſs of the climate, and out of the cloſeneſs and rough woody ſtate of the orchards; in which, it were next to impoſſible, to collect dry fruit; unleſs in a remarkably dry ſeaſon.

The *maturation* of the fruit, in the ordinary practice of the Diſtrict, is carried on in large heaps, in the open air, or in the pound houſe, or other covered ſituation *; where they remain, until they be ſufficiently "come;" that is, until the *brown rot* has begun to take place.

3. BREAKING. Formerly, this operation

* Preparing a flooring of rough ſtones, as mentioned above, is very judicious, when apples are matured in the open air; not only as keeping the baſe of the heap dry; but as communicating, perhaps, a ſupply of air, to the lower and central parts of the heap.

ration was performed *by hand:* a practice which is ſtill continued, I underſtand, in ſome parts of Cornwall. The apples being thrown into a large trough or tub, five or ſix perſons, ſtanding round the veſſel, "pounded" them *, with large clubſhaped wooden peſtils, whoſe ends are guarded, and made rough, to lay hold of the apples the better, with the heads of nails.

At preſent, the ordinary *horſe mill* of Herefordſhire, &c. is in general uſe, here: and it has the ſame objectionable point in its manufacture, as that noticed in the Glroceſterſhire mills: namely the coarſeneſs of the ſtone work. The *grinding* is of courſe imperfectly done †.

Lately, I underſtand, a *hand mill* has been introduced into this county, and is making its way faſt into practice; but it did not fall in my way to examine it.

4. PRESSING. The old *Preſs* of the Diſtrict, and which, I believe, is ſtill much in uſe,

* Hence, no doubt, the epithet "pound" is applied to the houſe, &c. in which the whole buſineſs of cider making is performed.

† See GLO. ECON. Vol. II. P. 333.

uſe, by the ſmaller growers of cider fruit, is very ingenious and beautifully mechanical. It is an improvement of the ſimple lever; by adding a rider, or lever upon lever; at the end of which a weight is ſuſpended. By this ſimple contrivance the acting lever is kept hard down upon the cheeſe, and follows it as it ſinks'! an advantage which no ſkrew preſs poſſeſſes.

As an improvement upon this (and with reſpect to power it certainly is ſuch) a *ſkrew* is made uſe of to *pull down* the looſe end of the lever; the other end of it, in either caſe, being moveable; and is fixed higher or lower, according to the height of the pile of pomage to be preſſed: lowering it as the pile is lowered by preſſing.

The laſt ſtage of improvement, or refinement, of the lever preſs; for ſuch it ſtill is, in principle; is to furniſh each end with a pulldown ſkrew; firſt the one end and then the other being worked, in the act of preſſing; a ſmall plummet being hung in the middle, to aſſiſt the eye of the workmen; leſt, by acting too long upon one end of the lever, they ſhould injure the worm of the ſkrew.

Theſe ſkrew lever preſſes are made of an enormous ſize, whether with one or two ſkrews: large enough to preſs four, five, or ſix hogſheads at once! the lever being equal in ſize to the deck beam of a man of war. Altogether an uncouth, unwieldy, monſtrous inſtrument.

The *method of preſſing* is invariably that of piling up the pomage or ground fruit, in "reed" (unthraſhed ſtraw) in layers; thoſe of pomage being ſome three or four inches thick, the reed being ſpread thinly over, and then another thin covering is ſpread acroſs the firſt. Under the gigantic preſſes above-deſcribed, the pile is four or five feet ſquare and nearly as much in height. On the top, a broad ſtrong covering of wood is laid; and, upon this, the lever is lowered.

A pile ſo large, and of ſo frail a conſtruction, requires to be preſſed with caution, in the outſet: a circumſtance which renders the operation extremely tedious: one of the enormous "cheeſes" of the larger preſſes taking two days to compleat the preſſing!

The pile having acquired ſufficient firmneſs, the outſides are pared off, ſquare, with a hay a hay knife; cutting off all the loose spongy parts which evaded the pressure, and piling them upon the top of the cheese, to receive the immediate action of the press: or are reserved for "beverage;" being watered and pressed separate *.

5. The MUST, or expressed liquor, which comes off, from this mode of pressing, is extremely foul, compared with that, which is strained through hair cloths. It is, therefore, placed in large vessels or cisterns, for its feculencies to subside, before it be put into casks.

6. In the FERMENTING of Fruit Liquor, nothing of superior excellence, I believe, is to be learnt, from the ordinary practice of this District. In the fermenting room of a farm, which has long been famous for its cider, I have seen an experienced manager, who has for several years had the care of this cider,—racking "one side of the house to-day, and the other side to-morrow," under a full conviction that it "would do them all good."

* For a description of the Herefordshire Press, and the method of pressing in Haircloth, see GLO. ECON. Vol. II. Page 312. and 340.

good." Under management like this, it muſt, of courſe, be mere matter of chance, if a caſk of palatable liquor be produced. But cider of a ſuperior quality being produced, as it were accidentally, under this ignorant treatment, it ſhews plainly how much might be done (indeed has been done *) by knowledge and attention. However, while the conſumption remains with the Diſtrict, and while ſtrength is the great recommendation of the liquor, ſuch knowledge and attention might, in ſome meaſure, be thrown away.

7. The FERMENTED LIQUOR is laid up in HOGSHEADS, of *ſixtythree gallons each*; or in PIPES, or " double hogſheads."

8. The QUANTITY OF PRODUCE is not more than ſupplies the conſumption of the Diſtrict; of courſe,

9. The MARKETS for ſale cider are the *towns*, and the *public houſes* of the Diſtrict; the *farmer's own conſumption* being ſupplied by windfall fruit; by the waſhings of the " mock," or pomage, in ſcarce years; and by inferior cider.

The

* Particularly by Mr. STAPLETON.

The *price* of marketable cider, on a par of years, has been fifteen ſhillings a hogſhead (of 63 gallons) for the muſt or unfermented liquor; and a guinea for fermented cider; which ſometimes riſes to two or three guineas a hogſhead: and on the other hand, ſome years the muſt has been ſold at five ſhillings, a hogſhead, at the preſs.

GENERAL OBSERVATIONS ON ORCHARDS AND FRUIT LIQUOR. There prices, conſidering the ſmallneſs of the meaſure, compared with that of Herefordſhire, make cider a more advantageous article of produce, here, than in the Mayhill Diſtrict; and, in ſuitable ſituations; as on the rugged ſides of vallies, ſufficiently ſheltered from more cutting winds, there can be no diſpute about the ſuperior profitableneſs of Orchard Fruits, in a pecuniary point of view, to any other ſpecies of produce; and moſt eſpecially to a ſmall farmer, who attends perſonally to the whole buſineſs, and whoſe wife and children are his aſſiſtants.

Nevertheleſs, on larger farms, where the management is left much to ſervants, and where

where cider, under any management, is but a ſecondary object, the buſineſs of making it interferes with the more important concerns of huſbandry: even the buſineſs of harveſt, and ſtill more the cleaning of turneps, are too frequently neglected, to give place to fruit picking; and the breaking and preſſing are, afterwards, not leſs inimical to the ſaving of potatoes and the ſowing of wheat; which, as has been ſhewn, requires all the hand labour the farm can afford. Beſides, the "dreſſing" which ought to be applied to the arable lands, it is to be feared, is too frequently beſtowed on the Orchard Grounds—for "how can dreſſing be beſtowed to ſo good a purpoſe."

Again, the drunkenneſs, diſſoluteneſs of manners, and the diſhoneſty of the lower claſs might well be referred, in whole or in great part, to the baleful effects of cider; which workmen of every deſcription make a merit of ſtealing: and, what is noticeable, the effects of cider, on working people, appears to be different from that of malt liquor. Give a Kentiſh man a pint of ale, and

and it ſeems to invigorate his whole frame: he falls to his work again, with redoubled ſpirit. But give a Devonſhire man as much, or twice as much cider, and it appears to unbrace and relax, rather than to give cheerfulneſs and energy to his exertions.

Another more flagrant evil, which is laid to the charge of cider, is the *Devonſhire colic*, analogous with the colic of Poitou. This violent diſorder has been aſcribed to the circumſtance of the mills and preſſes, of Devonſhire, having lead made uſe of in their conſtruction: and, under this idea, one of the preſſes, I had an opportunity of examining, was ſcrupulouſly formed without lead; the joints of the "vat" or bed of the preſs, being caulked with wool and cow dung, which is found to be fully effective, in this intention. But, in evidence of the improbability of lead being the cauſe of this miſchief, a mill, which had been conſtructed a century at leaſt, and which is cramped together by means of lead, being examined, it was found that no corroſion of the lead had taken place; even the marks of the hammer remained perfectly diſtinct.

This

This fact I do not ſpeak to from perſonal examination; but I received it from an authority, on which I have every reaſon to rely.

From two or three ſtriking caſes of this diſorder, to which I had an opportunity of paying ſome attention, it appeared to me to be the joint effect of cider, and of a vile ſpirit which is drawn, by the houſewives of Devon, from the grounds and lees of the fermenting room. Theſe dregs are diſtilled (of courſe illegally) by means of a porridge pot, with a tin head fixed over it, and communicating with a ſtraight pipe, paſſing through a hogſhead of water; the liquor being paſſed twice through this imperfect apparatus. It, of courſe, comes over extremely empyreumatic; and is drank in a recent ſtate, under the appropriate name of "neceſſity."

The patient having brought on, by an inordinate uſe of rough corroſive cider, and by the quantity of acid thrown into the habit, a fit of the ordinary colic, has recourſe to "neceſſity," in order to remove the complaint. The conſequence is an obſtinate

obſtinate coſtiveneſs, which generally continues for ſeveral days, attended with the moſt excruciating pain: and, though the firſt paroxyſm is ſeldom fatal, repetitions of it too frequently are: firſt bringing on a loſs of the uſe of the limbs, particularly of the hands, and, finally ending in the loſs of life; if the deprivation of life can be ſaid to be a loſs, under circumſtances ſo diſtreſsful.

Notwithſtanding, however, the accumulation of evils ariſing from the production, uſe, and abuſe of cider, the men of Devon are more ſtrongly attached to it, even than thoſe of Herefordſhire. Their Orchards might well be ſtyled their Temples, and Apple Trees their Idols of Worſhip.

It is not my intention, or wiſh, to depreciate the Devonſhire Orchards below their real value; but to endeavour to fix them at a proper ſtandard: to lower them ſo far, in the eſtimation of owners and occupiers, as to prevent their interfering too much with the more important operations of Agriculture. I wiſh to ſee them confined to unculturable ſites, and to have them conſidered,

considered, as they really are, a subordinate object of husbandry; in order that the occupiers of lands may bend their attention, with greater energy and effect, to the arable and grassland managements: more especially to the watering of meadows; and, of course, to the removal of many of the present Fruit Trees: changing them for a more certain, and, on a par of years, a more profitable species of produce.

23.

HORSES.

THE native BREED, which are still seen on the mountains that overlook this District, are very small: much resembling the Welch and Highland Breeds; and like them are valuable for particular purposes. The "PACK HORSES," or ordinary sort found in the inclosed country, are of a similar nature; but larger. The SADDLE HORSES, at present in use, are chiefly, I believe,

believe, brought into the Diſtrict, from the Eaſtward. Of CART HORSES, no breed can yet be ſaid to be eſtabliſhed. See BEASTS OF LABOR.

The BREEDING of Horſes does not enter much into the practice of this Diſtrict; except on the ſkirts of the mountains.

24.

CATTLE.

THIS Species of Liveſtock are entitled to every attention, in a Regiſter of the RURAL ECONOMY of the WEST OF ENGLAND. The Breed of Devonſhire is, in many reſpects, the moſt perfect Breed of Cattle in the Iſland.

The Breed,
Breeding,
Rearing, and
Fatting, of Cattle,

will require to be ſpoken of in detail.

I. In

I. In BREED, they are of the MIDDLE-HORNED Clafs. There are numberlefs individuals of the Devonfhire Breed fo perfectly refembling the Breed of HEREFORDSHIRE, in frame, colour, and horn, as not to be diftinguifhable from that celebrated Breed; except in the greater cleannefs of the head and fore quarters; and except in the inferiority of fize. The Cattle of Devonfhire refemble thofe of SUSSEX; except in their greater fymmetry of frame, and their being much cleaner in the fore-end, and every where freer from offal, than the ordinary Breed of Suffex. The Devonfhire Cattle refemble very much, in color, horn, cleannefs, and fymmetry of frame, a few of the more perfect individuals of the native Cattle of NORFOLK; but exceed them greatly in point of fize. They are a mean between the Norfolk and the Herefordfhire; fome individuals approaching towards the former, others towards the latter; but, taken in general throughout the county, they approach much nearer the Herefordfhire than the Norfolk, with refpect to fize: being fimilar, in this and other

other reſpects, to the breeds of Glocestershire and South Wales.

Theſe ſeveral breeds I conceive to have ſprung from the ſame ſtock. Their colour apart, they perfectly reſemble the wild cattle which are ſtill preſerved in Chillingham Park, in Northumberland; a Seat of the Earl of Tankerville: and it appears to me, that the different breeds, above noticed, are varieties, ariſing from ſoils and management, of the NATIVE BREED OF THIS ISLAND. A race of animals, which, it is highly probable, once ranged it, in a ſtate of nature; as the buffalo does, at this day, the ſavage regions of North America. The black mountain breeds of Scotland and Wales appear to me, evidently, to be from the ſame race; agreeing in everything, but colour, with the red breeds that are here adduced. The *ſhorthorned breed*, it is well known, were imported from the Continent; and the *longhorned*, it is more than probable, might be traced from Ireland.

The Devonſhire breed of cattle vary

much, in different Diſtricts of the County, both in ſize and mold. NORTH DEVONSHIRE takes the lead, in both theſe particulars; and its breed are, in both, nearly what cattle ought to be. In ſize, they are ſomewhat below the deſirable point, for the heavier works of huſbandry; but they make up for this deficiency, in exertion and agility. They are beyond all compariſon the beſt *workers* I have anywhere ſeen.

If they are to be ſtill improved, as WORKING CATTLE, it is by breeding from the largeſt of the North Devonſhire, or the cleaneſt of the Herefordſhire breed.

As DAIRY CATTLE, the Devonſhire breed are not excellent. Rearing for the Eaſtcountry graziers has ever, or long, been the main object of the cattle farmers of this county. Neverthelefs, I have ſeen ſome individuals of the breed, which evinced the practicability of improving them, as dairy ſtock.

As GRAZING CATTLE, individuals, in every part of the county, ſhew the breed to be excellent.

In

In WEST DEVONSHIRE, the breed is conſiderably ſmaller, than in the Northern Diſtrict; and their quality, in every reſpect, is lower.

In CORNWALL, the breed gets coarſer; with ſomewhat larger and more upright horns *: bearing a ſimilar affinity to the true Devonſhire breed, as the Shropſhire cattle do to thoſe of Herefordſhire: a ſtriking and intereſting fact, to thoſe at leaſt who find gratification, in obſerving the different varieties, and affinities, of this valuable ſpecies of domeſtic animals.

II. The BREEDING OF CATTLE. I had no opportunity of attending to the practice of North Devonſhire, in this reſpect. It is highly probable that a conſiderable ſhare of attention has been paid, for ſome time paſt, to the choice of males, if not of females, alſo; as it is not probable that accident ſhould have raiſed them to their preſent excellency.

 The

* Reſembling, in the turn of the horn, the wild cattle of Northumberland.

The Moorside farmers have little to answer for, in this respect; most of the calves, they rear, are purchased; either from the "In-country" farmers of their respective neighbourhoods, or are fetched from a distance: the calves of the dairy farms of East Devonshire and even Dorsetshire, are, I understand, bought, in great numbers, by the farmers on the skirts of Dartmore. The few which are bred, by these farmers, are, as far as my own observations have gone, of a small, clean, hardy sort; adapted to mountain pasture.

In *this* District (West Devonshire) the business of breeding cattle is conducted on the worst of bad principles. If a calf, which otherwise would be reared, discover symptoms of a fattening quality, it is "bussed;" suffered to run with the cow, ten or twelve months, in the manner of the *running calves* of Norfolk *; and is then butchered. If a calf of this description fortunately escapes so untimely a fate; but should show an inclination to get fat at two

* See NORF. ECON. Vol. II. Page. 121.

two years old, it is indulged in its propensity. It follows, of courſe, that the individuals which reach the ſtage of maturity, and from which new generations are to be raiſed, are, as to fatting quality, the mere refuſe of the breed: and nothing, but a ſtrongly rooted inherent excellency of quality, could preſerve them in the ordinary ſtate, in which they are at preſent found.

III. In the REARING OF CATTLE, I collected nothing, in this Diſtrict, which is entitled to eſpecial notice. The firſt year, the calves are kept within the incloſures; but, the next, are generally ſent to the commons and hill paſtures. Heifers are brought into milk at two and a half to four years old; according to circumſtances. And ſteers are broke into the yoke, at ſimilar ages; according to their ſize and keep.

What ſteers the Moorſide farmers do not want for their own work, are ſold to the In-country farmers, who work them ſometimes to eight, ten, or twelve years old. When thrown up, they are principally ſold to jobbers, or graziers, from the Somerſetſhire ſide of the county.

Thus a calf, dropt in the dairy Diſtrict of Eaſt Devonſhire or Dorſetſhire, may be nurſed at the foot of Dartmore, and reared on its hills; worked in Weſt Devonſhire or its environs; and driven back, through his native country, to be finiſhed on the marſhes of Somerſetſhire, for the London market.

IV. FATTING CATTLE. A portion, however, of the cattle reared in this country are fatted in it, or rather brought forward in fleſh, for its own conſumption. I did not ſee what in Smithfield would be called a fat bullock, in the country; except ſome two or three which were finiſhed, by a ſpirited individual, with the commendable view of appearing at the head of his profeſſion, both as a grazier and a butcher; and his praiſeworthy exertions ſhowed, plainly, what the cattle of Devonſhire are capable of, under judicious and ſpirited management.

Weſt Devonſhire, however, is not a grazing

grazing Diſtrict. Except ſome of the lands of Mylton Abbots, Lamerton and Taviſtock, and theſe are confined within a narrow compaſs, the ſoil is too weak for grazing. Its lands, in general, are better adapted to the purpoſe of bringing cattle forward, for aftergraſs, turneps, or oilcake, than for finiſhing them for market.

A peculiarity of practice in the SLAUGHTERING OF CATTLE, in this Diſtrict, muſt not be left unnoticed. In moſt parts of the Iſland, it is cuſtomary for butchers to bleed calves, previouſly to their being killed. And a ſimilar cuſtom prevails, here, with reſpect to bullocks. Enquiring, of an experienced and intelligent butcher, the motive for ſo extraordinary a practice, he gave a ſatisfactory anſwer. It aſſiſts in giving that deſirable brightneſs of colour, which attracts the eye, in purchaſing beef on the ſhambles; and what is of much more advantage to the purchaſer, it makes the beef keep better, in warm or cloſe weather; ſo that it operates as an advantage, both to the buyer and the ſeller And it is highly probable, that, in the ſummer

 ſeaſon,

ſeaſon, and for ill fleſhed bullocks at all ſeaſons, the practice might be found eligible, in other places. The trouble and difficulty of the operation, ſeems to be its greateſt objection.

25.

THE DAIRY MANAGEMENT OF *WEST DEVONSHIRE, &c.*

THE OBJECTS of the Dairy of this Diſtrict are

I. Calves.
II. Butter.
III. Skim Cheeſe.
Swine.

I. CALVES are either REARED; or are fatted, in the houſe, for VEAL; or are turned

turned abroad with the cows, as "BUSSES" or GRASS CALVES *: the laſt, a particular of practice, which generally pays amply; eſpecially when the moſt promiſing calves are choſen for this purpoſe. But the miſchievous tendency of the practice, in a general view, has been pointed out; and, conducted on the principles, on which it is here carried on, it cannot be too ſeverely reprobated.

II. BUTTER. The only particular of management, which requires to be noticed, in the Devonſhire Butter Dairy, is the ſingular METHOD OF RAISING THE CREAM; a practice which is, or lately was, common to Devonſhire and Cornwall. This peculiarity conſiſts in employing culinary heat, to aſſiſt in forcing up the cream, with

* Perhaps originally BOSSES, or WOOD CALVES (in contradiſtinction to HOUSE CALVES); namely, calves ſuffered to run with their dams, in the woods, or foreſt lands;—the practice and the appellation having probably originated, while the country was in the foreſt ſtate, and have both of them been continued, ſince the preſent ſtate of incloſure took place.

with greater rapidity and effect, than ſimply depoſiting the milk in open veſſels in the ordinary way, produces.

The milk having ſtood ſome hours, in broad pans or veſſels, either of braſs or earthen ware, it is placed in theſe pans over a gentle heat;—generally, over the wood embers of the ordinary hearth; but ſometimes over charcoal, in ſtoves fitted up for that purpoſe;—and remains in that ſituation until it approaches nearly to boiling heat: the proper degree of heat being indicated by pimples, or bliſters, which riſe on the ſurface of the cream. The ſmalleſt degree of ebullition mars the proceſs; which is therefore properly termed "ſcalding;" and the cream thus raiſed is termed "ſcalded cream," or "clouted cream;" probably from the tough cloth-like texture which it acquires by this proceſs.

The cream, thus raiſed, remains on the milk,—which is rendered very ſheer lean and *blue* by the proceſs,—until the dairy woman wants "to make the butter:" another ſingular operation, in the Devon- ſhire

ſhire dairy. The clouts or rags of cream being thrown into a large wooden bowl, they are ſtirred about, by a circuitous motion of the hand and arm, until the butyraceous particles unite; leaving a ſmall quantity of thick creamlike matter, or ſerum; anſwering to the churn milk of the ordinary butter dairy. In "ſcald cream dairies," no churn is in uſe.

The origin of ſo peculiar a practice may, perhaps, be traced back to the foreſt ſtate. After the arts of producing butter and cheeſe were diſcovered; yet while, perhaps, each family was poſſeſſed of no greater dairy than two or three cows; any proceſs which enabled the proprietor of ſuch a dairy to manufacture thoſe valuable articles, with a degree of certainty, was embraced as eligible: and how could a more fortunate proceſs have been ſtruck out, than that of ſecuring the milk and the cream from their natural propenſity of entering the different ſtages of fermentation, than the application of fire; which, at once, ſecures the milk from acidity, and the cream from putrefaction; until a ſufficient quan-

quantity of each can be laid up, for the purposes to which they are particularly appropriated?

But the disadvantages of this pristine practice are such as to render it ineligible, in the present state of cultivation. If, in the ordinary practice, the embers prove too weak, and an additional heat is required, fresh fuel is applied; and, if a scrupulous attention is not paid, the fatal ebullition takes place; and, in consequence thereof, the cream is too frequently mixed with the ashes. While over the fire, especially if fresh fuel be added, the surface receives the more volatile parts of the fuel, and perhaps a portion of soot; and after the pans are taken off the fire, while they stand in the kitchen or passages to cool, before they be returned to the dairy, the cream is liable to the depredations of domestic animals; and to receive, in a variety of ways, additional dust and dirt *.

In

* I am here speaking of the ordinary practice of farmers,—such as I have seen in the District: Gentlemen, and some dairy farmers, as has been before noticed, have stoves fitted up for this operation, which render the practice much more tolerable.

In Weſt Dorſetſhire, and the Eaſtern confines of Devonſhire, where the ſcalding of cream had been in uſe time immemorial, the practice has lately given way to the ordinary method of raiſing the cream and churning it; owing to the circumſtance of the butter of that Diſtrict having found its way to the London market; as will be particularly mentioned, in ſpeaking of the DAIRY DISTRICT

In different parts of Devonſhire and Cornwall, "raw cream dairies" are here and there ſcattered. Gentlemen, eſpecially ſtrangers who ſettle in the country, prefer "raw cream butter." That made from ſcalded cream has frequently a ſmokey flavor, and wants the even waxlike texture, obſervable in well manufactured butter.

Two reaſons may be aſſigned for the natives of theſe counties perſevering in the practice of clouting cream. Prejudice, or the attachment to eſtabliſhed cuſtoms, may be conſidered as one. The other is their attachment to "ſcald cream," as a delicacy, or article of luxury; in forming the "juncates," for which this country is cele-

celebrated; and as a favorite addition to paſtry of different ſorts; which is uſually ſerved up with clouts of cream. And, if the Weſt of England farmers prefer the pleaſures of the palate to the profits of the dairy, it might be extremely improper, in any one, to cenſure them, for continuing their preſent ſyſtem of dairy management.

SKIM CHEESE. I remarked nothing, in the manufacture of this article of the Devonſhire dairy, which induced me to regiſter the minutiæ of practice. In the dairy which I had the beſt opportunity of obſerving, the cheeſe was not *genuine*. However, from general ideas which I gathered on the ſubject, it is evident, that ſcalding the milk is not unfriendly to cheeſe; and it may be worth the trial, whether ſcalding ſkim milk in general, previouſly to its coagulation, would not be eligible.

26. SWINE.

26.

SWINE.

I. THE BREED, in this extremity of the Iſland, is the ſame long, thin-carcaſed, white kind, which has, pretty evidently, been once the prevailing, if not the only, breed of the Iſland *.

II. In the REARING of Swine, the moſt remarkable circumſtance is that of letting all the females remain *open*; and for a very ſufficient reaſon: there is not a Spayer, even of Pigs, in the Diſtrict of Weſt Devonſhire!

The FOOD of rearing Swine, while young, is the refuſe of the dairy, with turneps, clover, and even graſs, or ordinary herbage, *boiled!* A new idea, in the management of Swine. The food of larger ſtore Swine is

* See YORK. ECON. Vol. II. P. 235. And GLO. ECON. Vol. I. P. 316.

is chiefly grafs: they being not unfrequently driven to the fame pafture with the cows, and brought home with them, at milking hours: and are kept on, in this way, until they be two, or perhaps, three years old, before they be put to fatting! under an idea that the bacon of old hogs goes farther, than that made from young ones; not calculating the expence of keeping them to that *extravagant* age.

The native breed of the country, it is true, do not fat kindly, under eighteen months or two years old; but, through the attentions of the late Sir Francis Drake, the Diftrict is, at prefent, in poffeffion of the firft breed of Swine in the Ifland; namely, the beft variety of the Berkfhire breed: and it remains with the farmers to chufe whether they will perfevere in their prefent unprofitable breed, or adopt one which will leave more profit, by fatting, at nine months old, than their old fort will, at three or four times that age *.

III. The

* I have heard an objection raifed againft this breed of Swine, on account of the thicknefs of their fkins, compared

III. The method of FATTING SWINE, in this Diſtrict, forms another of the many ſingular practices which ſhew, that the Devonſhire huſbandry is not of *Engliſh* growth. They are ſhut up in a narrow cloſe hutch, in which they eat, drink, and diſcharge their urine and fœces; which are formed, of courſe, into a bed of mud, to ſleep in; their briſtly coats being preſently converted into thick coats of mail: in which filthy plight, they remain until they are ſlaughtered.

This extraordinary trait of practice is not to be aſcribed, wholly, to neglect and ſlovenlineſs; but, in part, to a principle of management, which, it is highly probable, has been drawn from experience. "Fat pigs ſhould lie wet; it keeps them cool: they are of a hot nature, and if they lie on dry warm litter, it melts their fat!" And, when applied to pigs ſhut up in a cloſe coop, without an aperture, perhaps, at

 which

pared with thoſe of the old white ſort; but this objection, while the hide of the hog remains a favorite article of human food, has no weight.

which to draw in a little cool freſh air, there may be much truth in this theory: which, however, would be ridiculous, if applied to hogs fatted in the ordinary practice of the Iſland; in which fatting ſwine have a cloſe room (be it ever ſo mean) to lie dry and ſleep in, and an open one, or little yard, to eat, drink, diſcharge, and breathe in. The advantage of raiſing a larger quantity of dung is, alone, a ſufficient recommendation of the latter practice.

The MATERIALS OF FATTING are *Potatoes*, with *Barley* or *Oats ground*, or *Barley boiled*. If fuel be cheap, and the mill at a diſtance, boiling the Barley may be as cheap and as little trouble as having it ground.

The BOILING OF HOG FOOD, which makes a part of the eſtabliſhed practice, in this Diſtrict, forms, at leaſt, a fit ſubject of experiment, in others. Where fuel is cheap, the practice may perhaps be found profitable.

27. SHEEP.

27.

SHEEP.

I. BREED. The ESTABLISHED BREED of the Country, whether we examine it on the mountains of Devonſhire and Cornwall, or in the cultivated Country which lies between them, is uniformly of the MIDDLE-WOOLED CLASS.

What is obſervable, however, in deſcribing a breed of Sheep, their HEADS are variouſly characterized: thoſe of ſome individuals are *horned*, others *polled*, or hornleſs —provincially "nots;" and between theſe there are, of courſe, individuals bearing a mongrel deformity of head, as if they were really a mongrel breed, of recent debaſement.

Neverthelefs, they have been, beyond memory, what they appear to be, at preſent. And what ſtrongly corroborates the idea of their being a diſtinct breed, they are found, on the Northern ſkirts of Dartmore, about OKEHAMPTON, of a diminutive ſize: not much larger than the heath Sheep of Norfolk. Yet, in uniformity of wool, in diſparity of head, and in their general appearance, their ſize apart, they perfectly accord with the larger variety of what may well be conſidered as the ANTIENT BREED OF THE COUNTRY.

It is obſervable, that, in the different varieties of this breed, there are many individuals which bear ſo ſtrong a reſemblance to the preſent breed of Dorſetſhire, as to leave little doubt of their having a natural alliance. And it appears to me moſt probable, that the horned Sheep of Dorſetſhire, &c. have been originally drawn from the antient breed of the Weſtern mountains; by breeding from a ſelection of the horned individuals. While a polled or hornleſs breed, now ſeen in the South Hams, may well ſeem, from their reſemblance, to have been raiſed, by a ſimilar ſelection, from the hornleſs individuals of the ſame antient ſtock. The encreaſe of carcaſe and wool, which

which they have acquired, is ſuch as would naturally ariſe from mountain Sheep being transferred to the rich ſoils, and genial climature, of South Devonſhire *.

The true Dorſetſhire (as they are called), or HOUSE-LAMB BREED, are found, at preſent, in great purity, in the Vale of Exeter, in Eaſt Devonſhire: of which

S 3 breed

* It may, with great ſhow of probability, be ſaid, that the Sheep of this Country are a mixture of the two breeds abovementioned. But from whence, it might be aſked, were theſe pure breeds imported? Where are the mother flocks? Suppoſing them to have been imported, and ſet down on the ſpots they now ſeverally occupy, it muſt neceſſarily have been ſome centuries ago, to give time to their mongrel progeny to mold themſelves to ſoils and ſituations; and it is very improbable, that, during the dark days of Agriculture, the two breeds ſhould have been preſerved diſtinct and pure, as we now find them; eſpecially the horned variety. Beſide, it will preſently appear, that the idea of their having been brought to their preſent ſtate, by SELECTION, is not only probable, but practicable.

Let it be underſtood, however, that what is here ſuggeſted, reſpecting this intereſting part of the HISTORY of AGRICULTURE, in this Iſland, is intended to agitate the ſubject, rather than to ſettle the point.

breed there are a few flocks, in *this* Diſtrict; but not of the pureſt kind.

The flock I found, at BUCKLAND, were of this deſcription: but were in a ſtate of neglect;—reverting faſt back to the native breed of the country, both in carcaſe and head! But there being ſtill a ſufficiency of the true breed left, to recover the flock from its degeneracy, it was thought more adviſeable to improve them, as the Houſe-lamb breed, than to change them for either of the more popular ſorts, that are working their way, even into this remote part,—namely, the SOUTH DOWN and the NEW LEICESTERSHIRE.

I muſt not omit to mention, by the way, a circumſtance attending the improvement of the Buckland flock; as it farther corroborates the idea of the horned ſheep of Dorſetſhire, &c. having been originally drawn from the antient mountain ſtock. In 1791, the flock, viewed in the aggregate, bore a much ſtronger reſemblance to the ordinary breed of the Diſtrict, than to the Dorſetſhire breed; eſpecially in head,—a conſiderable

derable portion of them being polled, or nearly ſo. Nevertheleſs, by a ſelection of females, and by employing males of the eſtabliſhed horned breed of Eaſt Devonſhire, there was, in 1794, ſcarcely a horned individual left, in the flock of five hundred: and, in that ſhort ſpace of time, a ſimilar alteration of carcaſe took place.

The two breeds above mentioned, are at preſent ſpreading, in all directions, over the face of the Iſland; and, in conſequence, other breeds will probably be neglected or loſt: and although, in many reſpects, theſe two breeds may excel the Dorſetſhire; yet they are neither of them ſuitable for the Houſe-lamb farmers; who may hereafter find it neceſſary, to give extravagant prices, for the only breed which will ſuit their purpoſe; and which may, therefore, turn out highly profitable, to thoſe who now preſerve it, in its purity.

Beſide, the Houſe-lamb breed, diſtinctly from that peculiar excellency, is, as grazing ſtock, a valuable breed of Sheep. The wedders, of the beſt ſort, fat perfectly well, at two years old; and pay, perhaps, in a middlesoiled upland situation, equal, as Graziers stock, to any other breed *.

II. BREEDING SHEEP. From what has been said respecting the heterogeneous state, in which the ordinary flocks of this Country now appear, it is not probable that much attention has lately been paid to the SELECTION of either males or females: and, yet, no Country in the Island would repay such an attention, better, than Devonshire; a principal part of whose lands are peculiarly suitable for Sheep.

The TIME OF PUTTING THE RAMS TO THE EWES is very early, compared with that of most other Districts. In the in Country, the middle of July is the ordinary time; the lambs, of course, beginning to drop, about Christmas; the month of January being the principal TIME OF LAMBING.

In the TREATMENT of Ewes and Lambs, I met with little observable, in this District:

* These remarks are not intended more to explain my own motives, for preferring an oldfashioned breed, than as hints to those who have similar flocks in their possession.

trict: kept graſs is chiefly depended upon, as the food of ſuckling Ewes. Turneps are ſometimes given to them: but it is found, here, as in other places, that although Turneps furniſh a fluſh of milk, and are beneficial to the Lambs, they do not, at the ſame time, afford ſufficient nouriſhment to the Ewes; which never fail to ſink in fleſh, when fed on Turneps alone. If, however, a ſmall quantity of hay were added, to correct the lacteſcent quality of the Turneps, this objection to them, as the food of ſuckling Ewes, would no longer lie.

The uſual TIME OF WEANING LAMBS is May or June; except for the late dropt Lambs, whoſe dams did not take the Ram in due ſeaſon. Theſe are ſuffered to run with the Ewes, and, if dropt very late, as in April, are generally conſigned to the Butcher.

Quære, May not a long continuance of the practice of breeding from the early dropped Lambs, and killing off thoſe which are lambed later in the ſeaſon, have aſſiſted in giving the remarkable propenſity or habit, peculiar

peculiar to the Sheep of this quarter of the Iſland, of admitting the male, at a time when the other breeds it contains are indifferent to the intercourſe of the ſexes?

III. STORE SHEEP. In the SHEPHERDING OF SHEEP, the particular which moſt merits obſervation, relates to the ſkill of the Devonſhire Shepherds in the training of their DOGS: and ſomething perhaps may depend on the nature or breed of theſe uſeful animals. Let this be as it may, I have not obſerved ſo much ſagacity, activity, and ſubordination, in the Shepherd's dog of any other Diſtrict.

This breed of dogs are ſomewhat ſhaggy, tall on their legs, and have very ſhort tails; the colors are various; but moſtly grizzled; ſome are of a ſort of dun color;—others—a larger ſmoother kind,—I have ſeen of a black color, marked with white.

The excellency of theſe dogs renders SHEEP PENS, in a degree, unneceſſary. If Sheep require to be looked over, or examined, as to be handled by the Butcher, or to be dreſſed, or cleaned, though it may require

require an hour's confinement, they are driven into a corner, and kept pent up there, by one or more dogs, until the buſineſs be completed.

If an experienced Shepherd wiſh to inſpect his flock, in a curſory way, he places himſelf in the middle of the field or piece they are depaſturing, and, giving a whiſtle or a ſhout, the dogs and the ſheep are equally obedient to the ſound; the one flies from him, with their ſwifteſt ſpeed, while the other, from every quarter, draw towards him in conſiderable haſte, long before the dogs have time to approach them. The ſtragglers are driven in, by the circuitous route of the dogs; which keep flying round, from ſide to ſide, until the flock be gathered round the Shepherd, cloſe enough, not only to be ſeen, but to be laid hold of, by him, if any thing wrong be ſuſpected *.

An objection would be raiſed againſt this practice, by the Shepherds of heavy, long-wooled Sheep; as tending to alarm, diſturb, and injure the Sheep; but little of this is in

* Are not theſe practices *French*?

in fact produced: for, being accustomed to it, from their earliest age, no alarm appears to take place. They will even follow the Shepherd about, as if they were sensible of his care and protection. Such being the effects of habit, over almost every species of the animal kingdom, when it is early induced, and when it is brought on by the example of parents, or intimates of riper years.

The SUMMER KEEP of Sheep, in the ordinary practice of the District, consists chiefly of the commons and rough pastures of the low country, or of the hills of Dartmore; to which Sheep are driven, in the summer season, from a considerable distance. Even some of the larger flocks are sent thither; especially, in a dry season, when the cultivated upland leys are burnt up. In WINTER, they are of course brought back to the inclosures; and to such keep as the Farmer can find for them. Snow seldom lying long, on the lower grounds of this District, very little hay, I understand, is given to store Sheep.

A striking feature in the management of Sheep,

Sheep, throughout Cornwall, and in the Weſtern Half of Devonſhire, is that of OMITTING TO WASH THEM, PREVIOUS TO THE SHEARING!

This practice, like many other practices in huſbandry, has its advantages and diſadvantages. In this caſe, the wool weighs heavier; but the price is lower, for "wool in the yolk," than it is for waſhed wool; ſo that it probably makes little for or againſt the grower; and, to the manufacturers, though it may require ſomewhat more labor in cleaning, there is a ſaving of ſoap, which more than makes up the loſs of labor. Wool which has been waſhed on the Sheep's back, requires ſoap, to cleanſe it properly for manufacture; but in unwaſhed wool, the "yolk;" or yellow egg-colored matter which is lodged among it, precludes the uſe of any additional detergent. Thus it becomes to the manufacturer a matter of no great importance, whether Sheep be waſhed or not.

It is obſervable, however, that wool ſhorn in the yolk, is liable to take a conſiderable degree of heat; a circumſtance which, if

made

made the most of, may be highly serviceable to the farmer; but the process of fermentation having ceased, it is probable, that not only the weight decreases very rapidly, but that the quality of the wool, loaded with so much dirt, likewise decreases. Beside, if the place of growth and the place of manufacture, be, as they too frequently are, distant from each other, the additional weight is an objection to the practice under notice: which, though it may be perfectly right, in a District which manufactures its own wool, cannot perhaps be generally adopted, with propriety.

IV. FATTING SHEEP. Little is required to be said on this subject.

The DESCRIPTION of Sheep, fatted, includes wedders, aged ewes, and common sheep, bought in for this purpose, by the in-country farmers.

The MATERIALS OF FATTING are grass,—particularly the aftergrass of young leys,—turneps, &c. The MARKET, chiefly Plymouth and its environs.

RABBITS.

28.

RABBITS.

I OBSERVED only one Rabbit Warren in this Diſtrict, which is now ſtocked; with a ſmall one, that has been diſwarrened. Nevertheleſs, there appears to me to be much land in the Weſt of Devonſhire, &c. which would pay better in a ſtate of Rabbit warren, than in any other ſtate of occupancy. I mean the higher weaker lands, and where the ſides of the hills have a ſufficiency of looſe rubble for the Rabbits to burrow in. The markets of Plymouth, and its Dock, would not fail to take off the produce.

An objection to Rabbits, in or near the incloſed country, lies in their being deſtructive to the large hedge mounds of this Diſtrict; in which they burrow, and become a ſpecies of vermin, difficult to extirpate;

tirpate; ſcooping out the inſide; where they make their lodgements; generally with an entrance on each ſide, and a third or perhaps a fourth, on the top. But if warrens were ſufficiently fenced in the York-ſhire manner, and the fences properly attended to, this objection would loſe much of its weight. The warren I ſaw, on the ſkirts of Dartmore, had no ſufficient fence to prevent the Rabbits from ſtraying.

29

POULTRY.

THE only circumſtance that ſtruck me, in Devonſhire, with reſpect to this petty article of Liveſtock, was the ſcarcity of Eggs, compared with the number of FOWLS. The markets of Plymouth, I underſtand, are ſupplied with eggs, in ſome conſiderable part, from the North of Devonſhire; from whence they are ſent, twenty or thirty

thirty miles, by land; and this while, to common appearance, there are a ſufficient number of Fowls kept, within ten miles of it, to ſupply all its wants of this article.

This circumſtance did not ſtrike me, until I had ſpent ſome time in Scotland; where, from no greater appearance of Fowls, the quantity of Eggs conſumed in the country, and the extraordinary quantity ſent, eſpecially from Berwick, to the London market, is almoſt incredible.

Theſe extraordinary facts led me to a cloſer inveſtigation of this ſubject, than I had, theretofore, thought it entitled to; and it evidently appears, that the whole diſparity of produce may be traced to a diſparity of management.

In Scotland, Fowls in general rooſt in the warm ſmokey cottages of their owners; are nurtured, and *forced* in a hot houſe. The conſequence is, they produce Eggs in every ſeaſon; and, generally ſpeaking, the year round. The Gentlemen of Scotland, ſeeing the ſuperiority of the Cottage Fowls, in their productiveneſs of Eggs, have removed the comparative ſterility of their own, by keeping them, literally, in HOT HOUSES;—built on a similar principle to those in which exotic plants are conserved: flues being formed in the walls; with niches or small recesses, on the inside, for the Fowls to lay and breed in: with roosts for them to rest on at night.

The same sort of fecundity is well known to be produced, by the warm livery stables of London.

On the contrary, in Devonshire, Fowls roost in the cool open air; frequently in trees; *in a state of nature.*

The Fowl, in its native woods, probably, bred only once a year; and, of course, produced Eggs at no other season; and, I think, we may fairly infer, that the nearer they are suffered to approach that state, the less fruitful they will prove.

DISTRICT THE SECOND.

THE SOUTH HAMS OF DEVONSHIRE.

INTRODUCTORY REMARKS.

THE knowledge which I gained, of this Diſtrict of the WEST OF ENGLAND, was collected in paſſing through it repeatedly, in my journies to and from Weſt Devonſhire; in an EXCURSION purpoſely made, in the autumn of 1791, to examine into its Natural Characters, and to mark how far its Rural Management differs from that of the Diſtrict, which circumſtances had aſſigned me as my principal ſtation; and in viewing a part of the DRAKE ESTATE, which lies within the SOUTH HAMS.

The EXCURSION was made from IVYBRIDGE, a rich and romantic ſituation, at the foot of the Dartmore mountains, to MODBURY, and KINGSBRIDGE; thence to TOTNESS and its fertile environs: from thence returning, by a different route, to Ivybridge.

In deſcribing the Natural Characters, and the Outlines of Management, obſerved in this Diſtrict, I ſhall, here, as on other occaſions, purſue the method which Nature and Science dictate.

GENERAL

GENERAL VIEW

OF

THIS DISTRICT.

I. SITUATION. The South Hams form the Southernmost point of the Department of Country, which is the subject of the present Volumes. Its NATURAL BOUNDARIES are Dartmore and the Heights of Chudleigh, on the North; Plymouth Sound, on the West; and Torbay, on the East;—the English Channel sheathing its Southern point;—its OUTLINE, or figure, being nearly triangular.

II. EXTENT. Estimating the base of the triangle at thirty miles, and its perpendicular at fifteen miles, we have an area of two hundred and twenty five miles; but if we include the rich valley of the Dart, which runs up towards Aſhburton, we may ſet down the extent of the South Hams at two hundred and fifty ſquare miles, or one hundred and ſixty thouſand acres.

III. ELEVATION. The tide flows up the eſtuaries,---with which the Diſtrict is deeply indented on every ſide except the North,---a conſiderable way within its area: nevertheleſs, the tops of the hills, of which the Diſtrict may be ſaid to be compoſed, are elevated conſiderably above the Sea. Viewing it with regard to Agriculture, it is truly an Upland Diſtrict. The bolder ſwells, towards the center of it, might be termed Heights; although, in compariſon with the Mountains that overlook them, they are Hillocks of a pigmy order.

IV. SURFACE. Viewed from even the midway ſtages of the Dartmore Hills, from whence almoſt every acre of the South Hams is diſtinctly ſeen, the Surface appears flat, or barely furrowed with water courſes, ---a broad flat of marſhes, or an extent of low vale lands.

But

But in crossing the country, the Traveller finds endless difficulties, arising from the great inequalities of surface. It is billowy in the extreme. Some of the swells are nearly semiglobular. The South Hams are the Stroudwater Hills of Glocestershire, without wood,---or the most billowy passages of the Chalk Hills of Kent or Surrey, intersected with hedges. Round Totness, the ground is most strongly featured; being there divided by deep rivered vallies; and between this and the feet of the hills, a similar style of ridge and valley is observed; corresponding with that of the more Western District.

V. WATERS. The Hills of the South Hams, as those of West Devonshire, are well watered. Springs are seen to pour forth their limpid rills from the sides of the swells, and frequently from near their summits. The waters from these springs collect in the vallies, and form rivulets and minor rivers; five or six of which have their estuaries, advancing some miles within the area of the District.

The DART is a ſtream of conſiderable magnitude. The reſt mere brooks, at dead water; but ſwell into rapid torrents, in the times of floods. The YALM, at Ivybridge, is a mountain torrent of the firſt rank.

VI. SOILS. To convey the beſt idea, I am able, of the ſoils of this fertile Diſtrict, I will adduce the remarks which were made, at the different times of examining them.

IVYBRIDGE TO KINGSBRIDGE. The Soil uniformly fertile. The tops of ſome of the hills are rich grazing ground! Other hills are leaner and leſs productive. But I obſerved not a field worth leſs than ten or fifteen ſhillings, an acre. The whole ride is worth twenty ſhillings, on a par! much of it forty ſhillings, an acre, to a Farmer. The hill ſides are excellent corn land;---the bottoms rich meadows. Some little red ſoil is ſeen, in this ride.

KINGSBRIDGE TO TOTNESS The nature andappearance of the country are much like thoſe obſerved, between Ivybridge and Kingſbridge;

Kingſbridge; excepting a high ſwell or ſwells, the ſoil of which is much inferior to any, in the foregoing ride:—The produce furzey, inclinable to heath: one of the Chudleigh Hills thrown in here. Much red ſoil appears in this ride. The water of the road, in ſome places, red almoſt as blood.

ENVIRONS OF TOTNESS. The ſoil of theſe Hills is rich in the extreme,—even to their very ſummits! moſt rich grazing ground. Autumnal graſs, near a foot long, now reclining on the ground; as groſs, and as darkly green, as the autumnal herbage of the Vale of Berkley.

TOTNESS TO IVYBRIDGE. The ſoil ſimilar to that of the central and more Southern parts of the Diſtrict; but on the whole, not ſo good.

IVYBRIDGE. A rich plot of ground to the Eaſt of the Yalm:—a deep loam on a ſort of gravel: worth, to a Farmer, thirty or forty ſhillings, an acre.

SHERFORD ESTATE. The Country is at preſent ſo completely burnt up, with the inveterate

inveterate drought of this ſummer (1794), that no accuracy of judgement can be formed of it. The ſoil, in general, is evidently of a ſuperior quality. But judging from the preſent parchedneſs of the crops, ſome parts of it are as evidently too ſhallow: a defect which appears to be common to moſt of the lands of the South Hams.

GENERAL OBSERVATIONS. From the ſum of theſe particulars, it is evident, that the South Hams, with reſpect to ſoil, ranks high among the fertile Diſtricts of this Iſland. There are very few, of equal extent, to place in competition with it.

VII. SUBSOILS. In the South Hams, as in Weſt Devonſhire, SLATEY ROCK, and SLATE-STONE RUBBLE, are the prevailing Subſoils: with, however, a few variations in the former, which are not obſervable in the latter. A vein of LIME-STONE runs along the Northern margin of the South Hams; and, in different parts of its area, a deep red ochery LOAM is obſervable; and, at the foot of Dartmore, a ſort of GRAVEL is met with. But theſe variations

variations are only incidental; and it may be ſaid of this Diſtrict, as of Weſt Devonſhire, that its lands are clean and ſound, adapted either to corn or graſs;—inclining towards the extreme of abſorbency, rather than to that of retentiveneſs.

VIII. TOWNSHIPS. Some of thoſe on the Northern margin of the Diſtrict, at the feet of the Dartmore Hills, are very extenſive: a circumſtance which has probably ariſen from the unreclaimed ſtate of their lands, at the time they were diſtributed into Townſhips. But the more remarkable circumſtance of the lands of the area of the Diſtrict—of lands ſo dry, rich, and habitable as thoſe of the South Hams—lying in Townſhips above the ordinary ſize, may be more difficult to be accounted for. Perhaps, the beſt reaſons that can be aſſigned for it are, their having been kept long in a ſtate of open paſture, as their name would ſeem to import they were; and, in courſe, their preſent ſtate of incloſure and cultivation being of comparatively modern date.

IX. TOWNS,

IX. TOWNS, &c. PLYMOUTH and its Environs have the ſame influence on the Weſtern point of the South Hams, as they have on Weſt Devonſhire. And the ſea port of DARTMOUTH draws off ſome part of the produce of the Eaſtern quarter.

The more inland market Towns are TOTNESS, PLYMPTON, MODBURY, and KINGSBRIDGE: with ſeveral conſiderable VILLAGES.

X. INLAND NAVIGATION. The Eſtuaries, which have been mentioned, afford convenient paſſage to ſmall veſſels; and, perhaps, preclude the uſe of Canals, while the Country remains in its preſent ſtate. From Kingſbridge, conſiderable quantities of corn and cider are ſaid to be ſhipped off. Small maſt veſſels reach Totneſs. And Aunton Gifford, a finely ſituated Village, has its Eſtuary; which, however, like the reſt, is ſhrinking from the ſpot, where in much probability, it formerly gave riſe to the Village or Town, which it has now deſerted. But ſome rich marſh lands, which it has left in its ſtead, more perhaps than recompenſe the loſs.

XI. ROADS.

XI. ROADS. On the Roads, as on the Soils, of the South Hams, I will tranſcribe the extemporary remarks which I find in my journals.

EXETER TO PLYMOUTH. The Road, though generally too narrow, is in many parts exceedingly well formed, and well kept. The materials blue marble, and a hard ruſt-colored ſtone. In ſome places, the barrel of the Road might be termed the ſegment of a marble cylinder. But the lofty hedges, on either ſide, are not only intolerable nuiſances to the Traveller, whom they ſeclude; but, in many parts, are injurious to the Road. The Magiſtrates have, therefore, a double motive for enforcing the law; ſo far, at leaſt, as to ſtrike off the ſide boughs which contract the lanes, and overſhadow the Road; and, in ſuitable parts, as at the more abrupt bends, to keep the bruſhwood down to the banks;---at once to let in currents of air, to dry the road when wet, and to blow off the duſt when dry; and, at the ſame time, to diſcloſe the beauties of their Country to thoſe who travel through it. Beſide, by obliging their tenants to prune

prune the hedges of the *Roads*, they might ſee the utility of the practice, and might be induced to extend it to *Farm* fences in general*.

IVYBRIDGE TO KINGSBRIDGE. The Roads are moſt intricate; numerous, narrow, and crooked; and rendered ſimilar in their appearance, by the ſame tall banks, and taller hedgewood, which are common to the Diſtrict; and this without guide poſts to aſſiſt the ſtranger: eſpecially in the bye roads, where they are the moſt wanted. They are likewiſe moſt unlevel,---braving the ſteep, where ſide-long roads would be equally near.

ENVIRONS OF TOTNESS. The private Roads, to grounds, how ſteep! ſtraight in the face of the ſteepeſt part of the hill! Firſt, no doubt, foot paths; ſtill horſe paths. Some of them too ſteep, even for ſledges.

TOTNESS TO IVYBRIDGE. The Roads much better laid out in this, than in the other rides. They frequently lead along the tops of the hills, and wind acroſs the vallies. There is much level road, and little

* See the MINUTES on this ſubject.

little that is ſteep. This is a proper pattern for the other Roads of the South Hams; though it could not be followed in all. The materials ſtone; beaten tolerably ſmall,---and covered, when freſh laid on, with earth or rubbiſh, to ſoften and bind the rough materials. The almoſt only inſtance I have met with, in common practice, of this moſt eligible method.

XII. STATE OF INCLOSURE. The entire Diſtrict, ſome ſmall plots excepted, is in a ſtate of permanent incloſure; and moſtly in well ſized fields, with ſtraight fences; except againſt public lanes; which are in general winding; as if they had been formed to incloſe ſuch fortuitous roadways, as we ſee deviating acroſs foreſts, and other open commonable lands: a fact which renders it highly probable, that the Diſtrict was incloſed from a ſtate of common paſture; or from a ſtate of paſture lands intermixed with temporary arable incloſures; ſuch as have been already particularly noticed *

XIII. HEDGE-

* See Page 32.

XIII. HEDGEROWS. The DANMONIAN FENCE is common to the South Hams. High mounds ſurmounted by Coppice wood. Not a Hedgerow Tree or a Pollard in a hundred ſquare miles! As naked of Hedge Timber, as the recently incloſed lands of Leiceſterſhire. Perhaps the ſea air is an enemy to Hedgerow Trees. Or the high mounds of this Country are not fit to receive them. Or the liſe-leaſe tenure has an intereſt in preventing their riſing.

XIV. PRESENT PRODUCTIONS. Along the Northern margin of the Diſtrict, and on the ſteep rugged banks of the Dart, Plots of WOODLAND are obſervable. But ſpeaking generally of the South Hams of Devonſhire, they may be ſaid to be deſtitute of wood; except what grows on the Hedge banks. Yet the fuel of the Country is wood; and it is, I believe, abundantly ſupplied with that neceſſary article, from its Hedges: a circumſtance which would no longer appear extraordinary, if we were to calculate the proportional quantity of the lands of the Diſtrict, which they occupy.

The

The Produce of its FARM LANDS varies in different parts of the Diſtrict. Not only the bottoms or coombs, in every part, are kept in a ſtate of *permanent graſs*; but, in ſome parts, the ſides, and even the ſummits, of the ſwells, particularly about Totneſs, are preſerved in the ſame ſtate. And although I obſerved no extenſive plots, of ſuch lands, as there are about Mylton Abbots and Lamerton; yet, perhaps, taking the Diſtrict throughout, the proportion of permanent graſsland, in the South Hams, is equal to that, in Weſt Devonſhire.

XV. THE APPEARANCE OF THE COUNTRY. Notwithſtanding the extraordinary beauty of the ground, or natural ſurface, of this Diſtrict, it is far from being rich in picturable ſcenery. Square fields, and ſtraight lines of Hedgewood, how profitable ſoever they may be to the Farmer, and pleaſurable to a mind reflecting on their utility,—are not grateful to an eye, viewing them in the light of Ornament.

This, however, applies moſt cloſely to the area, or more central parts, of the South

Hams. The Northern margin is finely diverſified. In the valley of the Dart, about Totneſs, the views in every direction are fine. Compoſitions the moſt ſtriking might here be caught. Below Kingſbridge too, the ſcenery is fine. And from Modbury Church, in the area of the Diſtrict, ſome lovely views are ſeen: winding coombs, backed by the rugged ſcenery of the Northern margin, and diſtanced by the mountain heights of Dartmore. But an eye delighted with the wilder ſcenery of nature, will find, on the banks of the Yalm, above and below IVYBRIDGE, the fulleſt ſcope for its gratification.

XVI. TENANCY. Lifeleaſehold is the prevailing Tenure, or Tenancy, of the South Hams, as of Weſt Devonſhire.

XVII. POOR's RATE. An evidence of the miſchiefs which MANUFACTURES are capable of entailing on Agriculture, ſtands conſpicuous, at preſent, (1791) in this Diſtrict.

Some years ſince, a woollen manufactory, of

of conſiderable extent, was ſet on foot, at Modbury, and carried on with ſpirit, and with ſucceſs to the individuals who proſecuted it. But their end being anſwered, the manufacture ceaſed, and all the vice and debility, which it had drawn together, were left as a load upon the pariſh. The conſequence of which is, I am informed, the Occupiers of Lands, within the Townſhip of Modbury, are now paying five ſhillings in the pound, to the poor, while thoſe of the ſurrounding pariſhes, do not pay two ſhillings.

THE

AGRICULTURE

OF

THIS DISTRICT.

I. FARMS. Moſt of the CHARACTERISTICS of the Farms, of the SOUTH HAMS, appear in the foregoing Remarks, on the preſent ſtate of the DISTRICT at large.

The SIZES of Farms, here, are various; the South Hams reſembling, in this and other reſpects, the more Weſtern parts of this quarter of the County. Fifty pounds, a year, rack rent, is eſteemed a middle-ſized Farm. One hundred pounds, a year, a full-ſized one.

II. FARMERS. In a Country which is principally divided into ſmall Farms, it would

would be unreaſonable to look for many of that valuable order of men, who are uſually ſtyled CAPITAL FARMERS. At the fair of Plympton, or at the market of Kingſbridge, I ſaw no appearance of men of this rank in ſociety. Nevertheleſs, men of enlightened minds are familiarly ſpoken of. Indeed, from ſome modern improvements, which will appear in this detail, to have been introduced into the Diſtrict, we might ſafely conclude, without other evidence, that it poſſeſſes men, who think for themſelves, and act without the authority of their anceſtors.

III. BEASTS OF LABOR. Theſe are OXEN, HORSES, and ASSES: the laſt being not uncommonly uſed for pack loads.

The PLOW TEAM is four or ſix oxen; or four light, or two heavier oxen, with two horſes before them; or three, or in ſome inſtances, two horſes,—with a boy, or a man, to drive, or lead them!

A ROAD TEAM I do not recollect to have ſeen, out of the public road, between Exeter and Plymouth: and very few in it. PACK

HORSES, I believe, are the prevailing, or universal, means of transfer, whether of produce, of manure, or of materials in general.

IV. IMPLEMENTS. The WAGGON and the CART may be said to be wanting, in the South Hams; which, in this particular, appears, from everything I have seen and heard, to be behind West Devonshire. I have seen building stones carried on horseback along the finest road in the kingdom; close by the side of which they were raised; and conveyed to a neighbouring town, through which the road passes.

In the PLOW of this District, I observed no deviation from that of West Devonshire; except in the addition of a *foot*, in one or more instances.

V. MANAGEMENT OF FARMS. The only observable deviation, in the general management of the South Hams, from what may be styled the genuine DANMONIAN HUSBANDRY, lies in the proportion of corn crops to temporary ley grounds, on the

the lands that are ſubjected to an alternacy of corn and graſs.

In Weſt Devonſhire, the regular diſtribution has been broken, in ſome ſort, by the introduction of TURNEPS and POTATOES *. In the South Hams, the breach has been made ſtill wider, by the introduction of CLOVER LEYS FOR WHEAT, and the practice of ſowing WHEAT AFTER TURNEPS.

How long theſe practices have been introduced, I did not learn. But from their not having yet reached the more Weſtern Diſtrict, they are probably of modern date. And although I obſerved them in ſeveral inſtances, they are probably not yet introduced into the ordinary management, even of this Diſtrict.

The CROPS of the South Hams are the three corn crops of *Wheat*, *Barley*, and *Oats*. The *Pulſes* are ſparingly, if at all, cultivated in the Diſtrict. *Beans*, at leaſt, are imported, in quantity. Some *Turneps*, a few *Potatoes*, and *cultivated herbage*, form the reſt of its arable crops.

 VI. MA-

* See Page 137.

VI. MANAGEMENT OF SOILS. Nothing ſtruck me, in this department of management, as differing from the practice of Weſt Devonſhire. The ſame velling, burning, and one plowing of ley grounds for Wheat and Turneps are obſervable: with, however, in ſome caſes, an additional ſpecies of tillage, which, though partially uſed, throughout this quarter of Devonſhire, did not fall under my inſpection, in the more Weſtern Diſtrict.

This operation in tillage, has for ſome length of time, I underſtand, been practiſed here, under the ludicrous name of "tormenting." It is performed with a SUBPLOW* of many ſhares, which are fixed in a triangular frame, ſupported by wheels; theſe ſhares, or ſub-hoes, working a few inches beneath the ſurface.

The only inſtance, in which I particularly examined it in uſe, was on a ley ground which had been velled &c. for Turneps, to be ſown on one plowing: the tormenting being done previouſly to the plowing; for which

* See MINUTES OF AGRICULTURE, in SURREY.

which it is an admirable preparation; as not only ſeparating the roots of weeds, but breaking the ſoil, and rendering it the more obedient to the harrow. As a preparation for Wheat, to be ſown under ſimilar circumſtances, the operation ſeems to be equally eligible.

VII. MANURES. The ſame manures, and the ſame management of them, are common to the South Hams, and to Weſt Devonſhire. The uſe of SEA SAND is faſt declining. LIME is in full repute, and is managed, I believe, without deviation, agreeably to the method which has been deſcribed. And BEAT BURNING, though prohibited by ſome, is ſtill in high eſtimation.

VIII. WHEAT. A NEW VARIETY of Wheat has lately been raiſed in this Diſtrict, and is likely to become a favorite ſort *. This improvement, having been made

* For an accurate method of RAISING VARIETIES of Wheat or other grain, ſee YORK. ECON. Vol. II. P. 4.

made by a Farmer, or a Farmer's ſon, and adopted by profeſſional men, is a ſtrong evidence that the bonds of prejudice are at length broken.

SUCCESSION. *Burnt ley ground* appears to be ſtill the prevailing matrix for Wheat. But, as has been mentioned, *Clover leys*, and *Turnep lands*, are now more or leſs ſown with this crop.

The TIME OF SOWING. In going over the Diſtrict, in the latter end of October, I had an opportunity of obſerving this particular. Sowing was then commencing. But, in general, the lime and earth ſtill remained, in roof heaps, unſpread: and, in many places, among Turneps, uneaten off. Some Clover leys were then breaking up, and, in one or two inſtances, men and women were hacking over the plowed ground, to receive the ſeed *. November is probably the principal ſeaſon of ſowing. But it is thought "very well if they finiſh by Chriſtmas." Can this be right? Is the practice peculiarly adapted to the climature

* See P. 189

mature of the South Hams? Or is it purſued, to counteract the foulneſs of the ſoil *? Or is it merely a bad practice, that wants to be improved?

IX. TURNEPS. In the South Hams, as in Weſt Devonſhire, Turneps are ſtill univerſally grown, after temporary Ley; except a few that are ſown in autumn, on Wheat ſtubble. I met with no inſtance, nor could I hear of any, in which they were ſown after Wheat or Oats, of the preceding year, agreeably to the prevailing practice of England.

Nor did I ſee or hear of an inſtance, in which Turneps were cleaned, and ſet out at ſuitable diſtances, with the hoe, as in that practice.

X. GRASSLANDS. The SPECIES of Graſsland, here, as in the more Weſtern Diſtrict, are

Mowing grounds, or meadows; which are partially

Wheat ſtubbles, in general, were then in full herbage.

partially watered, throughout the District;

Grazing grounds, or rich upland pastures; which were remarked, more particularly, about Ermington, Aunton, and Kingsbridge; and, most especially, about Totness; and

Pasture grounds, or the ordinary temporary leys of the Danmonian husbandry.

In the MANAGEMENT of Grasslands, I perceived nothing which gave me reason to apprehend, that it differs from that of WEST DEVONSHIRE.

XI. ORCHARDS, &c. This is the principal fruit-liquor District of Devonshire. But, as I had so favorable an opportunity of making myself master of the Devonshire practice, in the place of my residence *, I had the less occasion to attend to it, in the South Hams: whose practice, from what I saw of it, is the same as that of West Devonshire; except in the greater atten-

* See Note, Page 214.

attention which is paid, in the former, to the proceſs of fermentation. But the Herefordſhire practice being ſtill far ſuperior, in this reſpect, to that of South Devonſhire; and having already given an ample and, I believe, an accurate detail of that practice, it is the leſs neceſſary to reſume the ſubject, in this place.

In the proportionate QUANTITY OF ORCHARD GROUNDS, the South Hams, in like manner, reſembles the Weſt of Devonſhire. A ſtranger, in riding acroſs the country, would not ſuſpect it to be a fruit-liquor Diſtrict. None of ſuch extenſive plots of orchard ground, as meet the eye, in travelling through Herefordſhire, &c. and in ſome parts of Kent, are ſeen in South Devonſhire. Nevertheleſs, the farms being ſmall, and each having its Orchard, the aggregate quantity is conſiderable. The trees being low, and confined chiefly to the vallies, and perhaps overtopped by tall hedgerows, account for the little ſhow they make.

A minutia of practice in the DISPOSAL OF

APPLES,

APPLES, for houshold purposes, may not be too trivial to notice. In the ordinary practice of the kingdom, they are sold by *measure:* but, here, not unfrequently by *number:* a shilling a hundred being esteemed a moderate price.

XII. CATTLE. The BREED is that of *Devonshire:* excepting a few, in the hands of individuals, of the *short horned* breed *.

The South Hams is not emphatically a BREEDING District. Corn rather than Cattle appears, to a stranger passing through the Country, to be the principal object of the Farmers of the South Hams. Many of the working Oxen, that are seen in this District, are doubtless purchased of the Moorside Farmers †.

XIII. SHEEP. I observed some considerable flocks, on the West side of the District; and smaller parcels on the East.

The

* See MIN. 5.

† See Page 245.

The BREED varies as to *head*. On the Eaſt ſide of the Diſtrict, particularly about Totneſs, I obſerved a thick-carcaſed, long-wooled kind, uniformly polled, and with mottled or grey faces *.

* See Page 260.

A RETROSPECTIVE

A
RETROSPECTIVE VIEW
OF THE
RURAL ECONOMY
OF
SOUTH DEVONSHIRE.

IN taking the foregoing View of the SOUTH HAMS and its Rural Management, ſome reflections have ariſen, which it might be wrong to ſuppreſs.

Viewing its ſtate of huſbandry, in the aggregate, and including the modern improvements of individuals, it approaches nearly to the medium of that of the kingdom at large The permanent graſslands appear to be moſtly well kept, and are many of them partially watered: and the lands ſubjected to aration are not ſtrikingly foul; nor do they appear, *ſuperficially*, to be greatly in want of tillage.

Neverthelefs, one who has been accuſtomed to the more fertile parts of Norfolk, of the Midland Counties, and of other fertile and well cultivated Diſtricts,—and to obſerve, in the autumnal months, the plenty which everywhere preſents itſelf, —the ſpacious barn, and well ſtored rick yard, with herds and flocks ſeen in every direction,—is ſtruck with the apparent deficiency of produce, whether of corn or of cattle, in travelling over the South Hams, at the ſame ſeaſon.

This apparent deficiency, is no doubt, in a conſiderable degree, owing to the ſmallneſs of the farms, and to the farmſteads being much ſecluded in the vallies. But ſimilar appearances are obſervable, in the fairs and markets of the Diſtrict. And I am of opinion, that its produce, at preſent, is far from being adequate to its natural advantages.

Viewing the Diſtrict of the SOUTH HAMS, and its PRESENT STATE OF HUSBANDRY, in in the detail; a few modern improvements, —chiefly perhaps of individuals,—only excepted; they perfectly agree with thoſe of WEST DEVONSHIRE. In SOIL, SURFACE, and ESTABLISHED PRACTICE, they may well be conſidered as the SAME DISTRICT; and the following remarks are applicable to the whole of the incloſed lands of

SOUTH DEVONSHIRE.

IT may be right to premiſe, that, notwithſtanding the apparent deficiency, in reſpect to produce, the lands of South Devonſhire pay a rent, equal to what would be eſteemed their fair value, in better cultivated Diſtricts. This ſeeming contradiction is to be reconciled, by the circumſtance of the Danmonian practice having no high-fed horſes to ſupport;—by the lowneſs of wages, and by the frugality of living, among working farmers;—by a ready market and much water carriage;—and, ſtill more, by the favorable circumſtance of lime being freely uſed, on a ſoil that is not yet ſaturated with the calcareous principle.

Among the numerous IMPROVEMENTS, of which this Diviſion of the Weſt of England is ſuſceptible, the following have occurred to me, in taking a retroſpective view of the foregoing regiſters of its preſent practice. Many of them are noticed in thoſe regiſters. But I think it right to bring the whole together here, for the greater eaſe of thoſe, who may be diſpoſed to promote the proſperity, of this favored part of the Iſland.

In the FORM OF FARM YARDS much is to be done; eſpecially in providing proper receptacles for dung; to prevent its moſt valuable parts from being diſſipated. In ſome few caſes, I have ſeen the water, from dung yards, led over graſslands. But unleſs a reſervoir be formed, to collect ſuch water, in order to throw it over the land, in a large body, its effects are very confined and inconſiderable. For hints on this ſubject, ſee the cloſe of the following MINUTES.

In the MANAGEMENT OF HEDGES, I am

am of opinion much improvement may be made, by pruning the ſides, ſo as to prevent their drip and ſhade from deſtroying the under growth of the mounds, and the crops on either ſide of them; as well as to promote the upward tendency and ſtrength of the wood, which grows on the tops of the mounds; whoſe ſurfaces, being limited, can only throw out a certain quantity of produce; and it is but reaſonable to conclude, that ſo much of the nouriſhment, as is ſuffered to be expended on the ſpreading outſide boughs, is loſt to the more uſeful ſtems, which riſe upon the top. See the MINUTES, on this ſubject.

A proper FORM OF A LEASE, for a term of years, appears to be much wanted; ſuch a form as will encourage improvements, and give encreaſing value to eſtates;—inſtead of that which is at preſent in uſe. The modern forms of NORFOLK, YORKSHIRE, and the MIDLAND COUNTIES, will furniſh hints on this important part of the management of landed property *.

 In

* See thoſe Forms, in their reſpective Regiſters.

In the application of lands to their fitteſt uſes, ſomething remains to be done. There are many ſites which would pay for PLANTING, and ſome, which are are now in a ſtate of woodland, that would pay for CLEARING. See page 59.

In the MANAGEMENT OF TIMBER, there is room for much improvement. See page 88.

The USE OF WHEEL CARRIAGES may be profitably extended to many of the farms, both of the South Hams, and of the more Weſtern Diſtricts.

The ordinary PLOW of theſe Diſtricts is ſuſceptible of very eſſential improvement: and the TURN WREST PLOW would be found highly uſeful, in cultivating the ſteeper lands of this broken hilly country.

But the greateſt improvement, which theſe Diſtricts appear to be capable of receiving, lies in the SUCCESSION OF ARABLE CROPS. The preſent practice of taking three corn crops in immediate ſucceſſion, as well as the paucity of tillage which the land receives for theſe three crops (and even perhaps the ineffective form of the plow!)

plow!), doubtleſs aroſe from the difficulty which was experienced, at the time this practice was eſtabliſhed, in the RENEWAL OF THE SWARD, after fallows, pulſe crops, or more efficient tillage. Even the practice of drawing the weeds of Turneps, inſtead of cutting the ground over with the hoe, may have originated in the ſame experience.

But now, that the art of CULTIVATING SWARD is known, and practiſed, ſuch a mode of procedure is become improper: for the cleaner the ſoil, and the finer the tillage, with the more certainty and effect may ſward be cultivated.

In the Midland Diſtrict, where the ſoil is retentive of moiſture, and where the Turnep crop, and breeding flocks of ſheep, are leſs eligible, than they are, on the abſorbent ſoils of Devonſhire, there is a better plea for perſevering in a ſimilar practice. See MID. ECON. Vol. I. P. 186, and the MINUTE there referred to; alſo Vol. I. P. 195: where the reader may find this intereſting ſubject diſcuſſed.

In the MANAGEMENT OF THE SOIL,

very much requires to be done. The firſt ſtep is to clear it from obſtructions of the plow; and the next to reſcue it from the dominion of weeds, to which much of it may well be ſaid to be, at preſent, ſubject. In other words, it requires to be WHOLLY RECLAIMED from a ſtate of nature and neglect.

This reclaim is to be effected, by FREE CLEAN FALLOWS; or FALLOW CROPS, whether of ROOTS, HERBAGE, or PULSE; according to the circumſtances of the reſpective lands, and the ſtate of foulneſs in which they are found.

Another obvious improvement, in the ſoil proceſs, is that of driving TWO OXEN, with WHIP REINS, in all the lighter works of tillage; carrying a width of plit or plow-ſlice, in proportion to the ſtate of the ſoil, and the ſtrength of the animals.

For inſtances in which theſe improvements were carried into effect, ſee the following MINUTES.

An evident and great improvement, in the FARMYARD MANAGEMENT, is that of bottoming the dung yard with mold: a practice

practice by which a rich ſource of manure, for graſsland, is obtained, without loſs of dung to the arable crops: or, if the mold be mixed up with the dung, in the ſpring, a moſt valuable compoſt is formed, fit, in the courſe of the year, for any purpoſe of Agriculture; and this at the trifling coſt of collecting the materials; which may frequently be done, by means of backcarriage; and always at leiſure times.

It is at leaſt an object of experiment, in this uncertain climature, to try the effects of EARLY SOWING, on clean reclaimed land.

The preſent method of SETTING UP WHEAT, in the ſtubble, in this country, is very ineligible, compared with that of the North of England. See page 170.

In the HARVESTING OF BARLEY AND OATS, eſpecially in a wet and backward ſeaſon, the practice of the Northern Provinces would, I am of opinion, be found very advantageous. See page 175.

The WINNOWING MILL requires to be introduced, forthwith, into general practice.

The TURNEP CROP of this country is, at

at preſent, diſgraceful to Engliſh Agriculture. The practice of Eaſt Norfolk is perhaps the beſt which this Diſtrict could adopt. For a minute detail of that practice, ſee the RURAL ECONOMY of NORFOLK.

In the MANAGEMENT OF LEY GROUNDS, ſomething is evidently requiſite to be done: many of them, at preſent, are ſhamefully unproductive. If the Norfolk plan of management were wholly adopted, and the duration of the leys confined to one whole year, ſowing them with Wheat the ſecond, they might with ſtrict propriety be mown for hay, the firſt year. But ſhould they be continued, as at preſent, in paſture grounds, during five, ſix, or ſeven years, every effort ſhould be made, to prevent ſo ruinous an operation from being neceſſary; or, if it cannot be wholly prevented, its injury ſhould be rendered as light as poſſible, by mowing early, before the taller herbage has had time to deſtroy the undergrowth, and injure its own roots. See the MINUTES.

The quantity of WATERED GRASSLAND may doubtleſs be much encreaſed; and the preſent

preſent practice of watering be very much improved.

Some conſiderable portion of the preſent ORCHARD GROUNDS, it is very probable, may be converted, profitably, into watered mowing grounds. And many unproductive ſites be converted, with ſtill greater profit, to Orchard grounds. See page 115.

In the treatment of the preſent Orchards, one improvement is moſt obvious; namely, that of training up the trees, in ſuch a manner, that yearling cattle may paſture among them, during ſummer; and Swine, the year through; except during the gathering ſeaſon. In the pruning and cleaning of Orchard trees, there is likewiſe full ſcope for improvement.

To the MANUFACTURING OF CIDER, the Devonſhire Orchardmen might bend their attention with profit, by turning their produce to the beſt advantage. Their ſoil, and their climature, eſpecially in a moderately dry ſummer, are more friendly to the apple, than thoſe of Herefordſhire or Gloceſterſhire. And, were the arts of manufacture as well underſtood, here, as in the

May-

Mayhill Diſtrict, I am of opinion, that the cider of Devonſhire would outrival that of Herefordſhire, at the London market *. However, while cider remains a mere article of beverage, at the tables of thoſe who indulge their palates, there is leſs encouragement to excellency of manufacture, than there would be, were it faſhionable, as a ſubſtitute for wine.

The South Devonſhire Huſbandmen however, have an object of improvement lying open before them, which will repay them, ten fold, for their attention, compared with any advantage that can ariſe from their Orchard grounds, or their fermenting rooms. This important object of their attention is the BREEDING of LIVESTOCK; whether Cattle, Sheep, or Swine.

I am of opinion, that the rental value of the lands, of this part of the County, may be encreaſed, exceedingly, by a due attention to the improvement of theſe three ſpecies of domeſtic animals, only. And ſeeing the facility

* For a minute detail of the Herefordſhire practice, ſee the RURAL ECONOMY of GLOCESTERSHIRE.

facility with which it may be effected,—ſince there are ſuperior breeds, of cattle and ſheep at leaſt, within the limits of the County,—there remains no color of excuſe for delaying ſo valuable an improvement.

Finally, I will beg leave to ſuggeſt, in addition to the hints which are here conſiderately offered, that if the Gentlemen of this Country, who have lately formed themſelves into a Society, for the purpoſe of promoting its Agriculture, will aſſiſt the PROFESSIONAL part of their Countrymen, in the eſtabliſhment of SUBSTANTIAL PRACTICES, inſtead of waſting their attention and ſubſcriptions, on theoretic ſchemes, and impracticable ſpeculations, their Country, for ages to come, may have cauſe of gratitude for their patriotic exertions

A LIST

A

LIST OF RATES

IN

WEST DEVONSHIRE.

Buildings.

BLUE Slates, at the quarry, 3s. 6d. a thouſand; for the ordinary rough undreſſed Slates, great and ſmall: running from 4 to 12 inches wide, and 8 to 18 inches long, when dreſſed. The large Eaves Slates—provincially "Rags"—ſome of them two feet ſquare, when dreſſed, are ſold at 2s. 6d. a dozen; rough, at the quarry.

The price of "dreſſing," or cutting Slates into the required form, is 20d. a thouſand.

The

The entire workmanſhip, of dreſſing, pinning, pins, and laying on, in mortar, is 6s. a ſquare, of 100 ſquare feet: without pins, 5s. 6d. a ſquare.

A ſquare of Slate roofing takes about a thouſand Slates.

Oak timber—15d. a foot.

Aſh timber—1s. to 14d. a foot.

Lime—5d. a buſhel.

Maſons' wages—18d. a day, and a quart of cider.

Carpenters' wages—the ſame.

Woodland Produce.

Cordwood – ſee page 95.

Rough Topwood—prov. "Sheedwood" (7 feet long, and the thickneſs of the arm, to that of the thigh)—3 or 4s. each 100.

Spray Faggots (4 feet long and 3 girt) 16d. a dozen to the King's bakehouſes, &c.

Hus-

HUSBANDRY.

The yearly wages of ſervants are,—

Prime Men Servants 8l.

Second 6l.

Women Servants 3l. to 3 guineas.

Boys 9d. to 15d. a week.

Day wages:—in winter and ſpring, 1s. a day; with a quart of cider, to conſtant laborers. In hay time, 1s. with more liquor. In harveſt, 1s. with full board. See alſo page 107.

Mowing meadow graſs—2s. Clover—20d. and Corn 18d. the cuſtomary acre *; with 3 or 4 quarts of cider, each acre.

Reaping Wheat—4 or 5s. an acre, without binding it.

Thraſhing Wheat (in the Devonſhire manner see page 181.)—1s. a "buſhel" of two Wincheſter buſhels; including the making up and binding of the reed.

* Customary acre. This is calculated by perches of eighteen feet ſquare; being proportioned to the ſtatute acre, nearly as ſix is to five.

Day's work of a packhorſe—1s.
Plowing ley ground—6s. an acre.
——— broken ground—4s. 6d. an acre
Agiſtment of a cow—2s. a week.
———— of ſheep—2d. or 3d. a head.
———————- for the winter—4s. from October or November to Lady-day: an extra price, which is owing to the facility of keeping ſheep, in ſummer, on the common and foreſt lands.

PROVINCIALISMS

PROVINCIALISMS

OF

WEST DEVONSHIRE.

A.

APPLE DRONES: waſps (the ordinary name).

ARRISHES: ſtubbles.

ARRISH MOWS: field ſtacklets. See Vol. I. page 171.

B.

BALLARD: a caſtrate ram.

BARKER: a rubber, or whetſtone.

BARTON: a large farm. See page 101.

BEAT: the roots and ſoil ſubjected to the operation of "burning Beat."—See Vol. I. P. 141.

BEATING AXE: ſee as above.

BEEN: a with, withey, or band: a twifted twig.

BEESOM or BIZZOM (*Spartium Scoparium*): the Broom plant: hence a name of the fweeping broom of the houfewife.

BEVERAGE: water cider, or fmall cider.

BLIND NETTLE (*Galeopfis tetrahit*): wild hemp.

BURROW: a hillock or heap; as "Stone Burrows"—"Beat Burrows:" hence, probably, Barrow—(*Tumulus*).

BUSS: a grafs calf. See page 249.

BUTT: a clofe-bodied cart; as dung butt, or wheel cart; gurry butt, or fledge cart: ox butt; horfe butt.

BUTT LOAD: about fix feams.

C.

CADDEL (*Heracleum Sphondilium*): cow parfnip.

CESS or ZESS: a mow, in a barn.

CHEESE: the pile of pomage, in making cider

CLAW-ILL: the foul, in cattle.

CLOUTED CREAM: cream raifed by heat.

COB, or COBWALL: mudwall.

CONVENTIONARY RENTS: the referved rents of life leafes.

COOMB: a narrow meadowy bottom; generally, or always, between hanging woods.

COURTLAGE: farm yard.

COUSIN-

COUSIN BETTY: a female changeling, real or counterfeit, who goes about the Country, to excite charity; as ſhe does in Yorkſhire,—under the ſame name!

CROOKS: a furniture of packhorſes. See page 121.

CROW BAR, or BAR IRE: an iron crow.

CULVERS: pigeons.

CULVER HOUSE: pigeon houſe, or dove cot.

D.

DASHELS *(Cardui)*: thiſtles (the ordinary name).

DRAGS: large harrows.

DRAY: a ſledge, for light produce, as hay or ſtraw. Q. A corruption of Draw?

To DRAW: to carry, or convey, hay or corn, on a waggon or ſledge: moſt proper. Q. From dray or draw—a ſledge?

DRUDGE: a large team rake. See page 125.

E.

ETH—is in common uſe, as the termination of the third perſon ſingular: HATH, DOTH, are alſo in ordinary uſe.

EARTH RIDGES: ſee page 158.

EAVER *(Lolium perenne)*: raygraſs.

F.

FAIRIES (pronounced "VAIRIES"): ſquirrels!

FERN WEB (*Scarabæus Horticola?*): a ſmall chaffer; injurious to the fruit of the apple tree, while very ſmall.

FETTER LOCK: fetlock of a horſe; by corruption, perhaps, Footlock.

FLAPDOCK (*Digitalis purpurea*): Fox Glove.

FRENCH NUTS: walnuts.

FRITH: bruſhwood.

G.

GALE: a caſtrate bull.

GREENSIDE: graſs, turf, greenſward.

GREY BIRD: the thruſh; no doubt, in contradiſtinction to the Black bird; both being birds of ſong, and nearly of the ſame ſize; a ſimple, apt diſtinction.

GURRY BUTT: dung ſledge. See page 121.

H.

HACK: a one-ended mattock.

HAM TREES: hames.

HAMWARDS: ſtraw or ruſh collars, for horſes.

HANDBEATING: ſee page 142.

HAND-

HANDREAPING: ordinary reaping; contradistinct from hewing.

HAUL-TO: a three-tined dung drag.

To HEAL: to cover, as with slates.

HEALING or HELLING: the slate covering of a roof; also the operation of slating: hence,

HELLIER: a slater.

HERBERY: a cottage garden, or herb garden.

HEWING: a method of cutting wheat. See page 168.

HINE: bailiff, or farm steward.

HOG COLTS: yearling colts.

HOGS: yearling sheep.

HOLM (*Ilex Aquifolium*): holly.

J.

JUNCATE, or JUNKET: coagulated milk; eaten in the undisturbed state of coagulation: with sugar, spices, and clouted cream.

K.

KEEZER: a sort of sieve.

L.

To LEAD: to carry "trusses," on horseback. See page 167.

LEAR

LEAR or LEARY: empty; as an unloaded cart or waggon.

LEAT: an artificial rill, rivulet, or brook. See Vol. II. p. 269.

LENT ROSE (pl. LENT ROSEN): the Narcissus, or Daffodil.

LINHAY: an open shed.

M.

MASTS, or MESS? Acorns.

MAZED: silly—idiotic.

TO MELL: to mix, as lime and earth.

MORES: roots, whether of grass or trees (the ordinary name).

MOCK: pomage, or ground fruit.

MOW: a rick or stack.

MOWHAY: stackyard.

N.

NECESSITY: a base kind of spirit. See p. 236

NOT or KNOT: polled, as sheep.

O

OAK WEBB (*Scarabæus Melolontha*): the Chaffer, or Maybug.

To

To ORDAIN: to order.

ORDAINED: intended (common).

OVERLAND FARM: a parcel of land, without a houſe to it.

P.

PASSAGE: ferry; the ordinary name.

PIKE, PEEK, or PICK: a prong or hay fork. Q. Analogous with war pike?

TO PITCH: to fling ſheaves upon a ſtack or mow. See page 177.

PLANSHER: a chamber floor.

PLOW: a team of oxen.

PLUM: light and puffy, as ſome ſoils.

POOK: a cock of hay.

POTWATER: water for houſhold purpoſes.

POUND HOUSE: cider manufactory. See p. 228.

POTTS: furniture of pack horſes. See p. 122

R.

RAW CREAM: cream raiſed in the natural way: not "ſcalded," or "clouted."

RED HAY: mowburnt hay; in diſtinction to "green hay," or hay which has taken a moderate heat; and to "vinny hay," or that which is mouldy.

REED: unbruiſed ſtraw, of wheat or rye.

ROO: rough.

SCALD

S.

SCALDCREAM: cream raiſed by heat; clouted cream.

SEAM: a horſe load; or three hundred-weights.

SFWL or SULE,—pronounced "ZULE:" a plow (the only name). See Plow.

SHEEDWOOD: rough poles of topwood.

SHIPPEN: an ox houſe.

SKIRTING: ſee page 144.

SKOVES: reaps, ſhoves, grips, or bundles, of corn;—unbound ſheaves.

SLAPDASH: roughcaſt, or liquid coating of buildings.

SLATAXE: a mattock, with a ſhort axe end.

SLIDEBUTT: dungſledge. See GURRYBUTT.

SMALL: low, as the water of a river, &c.

SOUANT: fair, even, regular (a hackneyed word).

TO SPADE: to pare, or breaſtplow.

SPARS: thatching rods.

SPINE: turf, ſod, ſward.

SPIRE *(Arundo)*: reed.

STAFF: a meaſure of nine feet; half a cuſtomary rod.

STEM: the handle of a fork.

STICKLE: ſteep, as a road; or rapid, as a ſtream.

STROLL: a narrow ſlip of land.

STROYL:

STROYL: couch, or other weeds; or roots of weeds: especially what harrow up, or rake out of the soil; whether in the field, or the garden.

SURVEY: a sort of auction. See page 71.

T.

To TILL: to sow and harrow in the seed; to seminate.

TONGTREE: the pole of an ox cart, or waggon.

TOR: a ragged pointed hill; as "Brent Tor," —"Roo-Tor,"—"High-Tor."

TORMENTING: sub-hoing, or sub-plowing. See page 296.

TRONE: trench or drain.

TRUSSES: bundles of corn or straw, to be "led" on horseback. See page 167.

TUCKER: fuller.

TUCKING MILL: fulling mill.

TURF: peat.

V.

VAGS: turves, for fuel. Q. A corruption of Flags? see PROV. of NORFOLK.

VAT: the bed of the cider press.

To VELL: see page 143.

VETTY:

VETTY : appoſite, ſuitable ; — oppoſed to WISH.

VINNY : mouldy.

VORRAGE: earth collected, for "melling" with lime.

W.

WANTS : moles.

WHITAKER : a ſpecies of quartz. See page 16.

WHITE WITCH : a good creature, which has the power of counteracting the evil deſigns of Black Witches. Such kind Spirits formerly were found in Yorkſhire : and are ſtill ſpoken of, there, by the ſame name !

WISH: inapt, bad, unfit, as " wiſh weather",—or any " wiſh thing",—as a ſtone, or a piece of timber, ill ſuited to the purpoſe for which it is applied or required (another hackneyed epithet).

Y.

YOKE of OXEN : a pair of oxen.

END OF THE FIRST VOLUME

Printed in the United States
By Bookmasters